WITHDRAWN

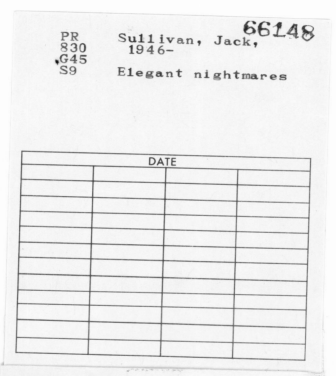

DATE			

I.C.C. LIBRARY

© THE BAKER & TAYLOR CO.

Elegant Nightmares

ELEGANT NIGHTMARES

THE ENGLISH GHOST STORY
FROM LE FANU TO BLACKWOOD

By JACK SULLIVAN

Ohio University Press
Athens, Ohio

Library of Congress Cataloging in Publication Data

Sullivan, Jack, 1946-
    Elegant nightmares.

    Bibliography: p.
    Includes index.
    1. Ghost stories, English—History and criticism.
I. Title.
PR830.G45S9   823'.0872   77-92258
ISBN 0-8214-0374-5

For Barbara

CONTENTS

ACKNOWLEDGEMENTS

I would like to thank Carl Woodring and Michael Rosenthal for their intensive criticism and encouragement. Their insights have been crucial not only in the preparation of this book but in the development of my general approach to literature. A very special thanks is due George Chastain, my cover illustrator and old friend, whose incisiveness as a critic almost equals his brilliance as an artist. His encyclopedic knowledge of ghostly fiction has greatly influenced my thinking and research. I have also been fortunate enough to know Ramsey Campbell, Jim Kent, T.E.D. Klein, Kirby McCauley, and David Bell—all exceptionally gifted writers and editors in the genre who have been generous with their advice. Finally, I am grateful to my parents, who have always supported even my less orthodox literary interests.

In the past ghosts had certain traditional activities; they could speak and gibber, for instance; they could clank chains. They were generally local, confined to one spot. Now their liberties have been greatly extended; they can go anywhere, they can manifest themselves in scores of ways. Like women and other depressed classes, they have emancipated themselves from their disabilities, and besides being able to do a great many things that human beings can't do, they can now do a great many things that human beings can do. Immaterial as they are or should be, they have been able to avail themselves of the benefits of our materialistic civilization.

—L. P. Hartley[1]

T. S. Eliot once complained that Yeats's only two interests during their early acquaintance were "George Moore and spooks."[2] That Eliot was haunted by "spooks" of his own is demonstrated by his collapse, first into a nervous breakdown and later into Anglicanism. As Hartley's delightful statement suggests, twentieth-century spooks "manifest themselves in scores of ways." Nevertheless, Eliot's reaction is important, for it reflects an embarrassment with Yeats's occultism which still is a commonplace in the academic world. Critics have labored diligently and ingeniously to concoct theories explaining away Yeats's earnest, lifelong interest in the supernatural. Rarely mentioned are Yeats's ghost stories, even though he published some fifty-eight of them.

Since (with one or two striking exceptions) Yeats's ghost stories are not particularly good ones, their obscurity is at least partially deserved. Consisting chiefly of Irish folk tales retold in the affectedly "simple English" of Lady Gregory, they are effective propaganda for the Celtic revival of the nineties, but little else. The marriage of self-conscious simplicity and swooning eloquence in Yeats's prose style is not a happy one, particularly for ghost stories. What *is* important is that a figure of Yeats's stature would write these stories

1

(not to mention his many ghostly poems) and take them seriously. At the turn of the century, supernatural chillers were very much the fashion. Several major English writers—including Conrad, James, Hardy, and Forster—turned out supernatural tales. Some of these, such as Hardy's "The Withered Arm," James's "The Turn of the Screw," and Conrad's "The Idiots" show considerable care, control, and ingenuity; they are minor masterpieces by major artists. Given the quality of the prose, it is reasonable to conjecture that these writers did not see themselves as slumming when they wrote tales of terror.

In a sense, the ghost story represents the most concrete (if somewhat vulgarized) manifestation of definitive trends in the major fiction of Lawrence, Joyce, Conrad, Hardy and Woolf: the fascination with darkness and irrationality, the focus on unorthodox states of consciousness and perception, the projection of apocalypse and chaos, and above all the preoccupation with timeless "moments" and "visions." As developed by Sheridan Le Fanu, the English ghost story offered a trim, ready-made apparatus for all of these themes. Narrators and characters in ghost stories always confront darkness and irrationality; the narrator usually seems to think that how something is seen is more significant than what is seen. At the same time, the characters really see things; they have visions and epiphanies which change everything.

The contributions of major writers to the ghost story constitute only a small part of a remarkable eruption of ghostly tales which began in the late nineteenth century and continued unabated through World War I. I am concerned with the efforts of specialists, beginning with Le Fanu, who contributed the bulk of these tales and mapped out the boundaries of supernatural horror in English fiction. A complete list of these writers—including those who produced tales on an occasional basis after the war—would be formidable. E. F. Benson, M. R. James, Oliver Onions, L. P. Hartley, Arthur Machen, Algernon Blackwood, Arthur Quiller-Couch, A. C. Benson, William F. Harvey, William Hope Hodgson, Walter de la Mare, E. G. Swain, R. H. Malden, Cynthia Asquith, Rudyard Kipling, Robert Louis Stevenson, Bram Stoker, Charlotte Riddell, May Sinclair, and many others would be on it.

There has been occasional speculation about why ghost stories proliferated during this period, most of it an appendage of the larger question of the Edwardian obsession with ghostly societies, experiments, and manifestoes. The apocalyptic quality of these stories—the sense of a gradual building of uncontainable forces—is part of a spirit of dissonance and restlessness embodied in such diverse forms as the music of Stravinsky, the fiction of Huysmans, and the essays of Freud. Like so much art of the transitional period between the late nineteenth century and World War I, the tale of terror was symptomatic of a cultural malaise which some historians view as a premonition of the Great War.[3] The recent American interest in all things occult and horrific may possibly grow out of a similar fetish for disaster occasioned initially by the escalation of Vietnam and Watergate: when things appear to be falling apart, supernatural horror stories provide their authors and readers with a masochistic, but relatively safe means of fantasizing the worst.

The most interesting historical speculation about the growth of these stories in relation to the culture that spawned them is found in Samuel Hynes's *The Edwardian Turn of Mind*. Hynes views the ghost story as one aspect of a cultural crisis which impelled artists into increasingly bizarre and subjective modes of expression. He contends that the ghostly tale is the fictional counterpart of William James's attempts to yoke religious experience with apparitions, hallucinations, and mind-changing drugs. He also sees the ghost story as a reaction against the sprawling realism of Dickens and Thackeray: "After the social realism of the Victorians, from Dickens to George Moore, Edwardian novelists (some of them, at any rate) turned toward the mysterious and the unseen, just as the psychic researchers turned from the natural sciences to spiritualism."[4]

Most of the commentary on causes, however, is typified by Philip Van Doren Stern's assessment:

> Fine stories were written before and since that time [the turn of the century], but never has there been such a flood of them within so short a period. . . . It is not easy to understand why this brief period at the turn of the century was so rich. Perhaps one clue lies in the fact that it marked the beginning of science's dominance of the world.

It was then that the automobile began to replace the horse; man
first learned to fly; and he found out how to talk through space
and look through solid substance. Before such miracles, ancient ways
of thinking went down. A fierce, new technological civilization then in
in the throes of birth was to bring horrors of its own upon mankind.
Skepticism and disillusionment followed in the wake of wars and violent upheavals. Like the beginners of the Romantic movement, the
men who were writing the supernatural literature of the early years
of the century probably did not know that they were singing the swan
song of an earlier way of life.[5]

Virtually every supernatural fiction anthology contains a variation on this statement, perpetuating the notion that ghost
stories represent a fond, fireside vision of the nineteenth
century, "a swan song of an earlier way of life." One of the
questions I address myself to in this study is whether this is
so—or whether ghost and horror stories embody that very
"skepticism" they allegedly combat. Do ghost stories belong
in the twentieth century or are they, like the music of Rach-
maninoff, endearing throwbacks?

Stern's sentimentalizing is closely related to a more sophisticated argument frequently advanced by apologists for orthodox Christianity. T. S. Eliot, a ghost story fan, states that
supernatural horror stories become "inferior" when the
"supernatural world is not really believed in, but is merely
exploited for an immediate but very transient effect on the
reader."[6] Russell Kirk carries the argument a few steps
further. Stating that ghost stories preserve "hierarchical"
Christian values, he goes on to interpret the "truth" of this
"innately conservative" form: "Now it can be said of the
better ghostly tale that it is underlain by a sound concept of
the character of evil. Defying nature, the necromancer conjures up what ought not to rise again this side of Judgment
Day. But these dark powers do not rule the universe; they are
in rebellion against natural order; and by bell, book and
candle, literally or symbolically, we can push them down
under."[7] One of my main projects is to see whether these
stories imply a "natural order" in the universe and whether
the horrors they unleash are such that "we can push them
down under." Is it true, as Edmund Wilson claims, that these
"injections of imaginary horror . . . soothe us with the mo-

mentary illusion that the forces of madness and murder will be tamed?"

One of the most original statements made about the question of "belief" in these stories comes from a surprisingly early and unlikely source: H. P. Lovecraft in his 1927 essay, "Supernatural Horror in Literature." Lovecraft's view, the inversion of Eliot's and Kirk's, is that "materialists" write the most frightening stories. The writer who denies the existence of the supernatural sees in the supernatural invasion "an absolute and stupendous violation of the natural order" whereas the believer views the supernatural as a natural, "commonplace" phenomenon.[9] My interest is not in whether a given writer is a thorough-going skeptic (although several were), but in whether the literature tends to present the supernatural as an ominous validation of a suspected "violation" in the cosmos. Taking this question a step further, I am interested in whether the ghostly experience points toward a fundamentally disordered universe. This is a crucial question, and one which has not been explored.

There have been other studies of English ghost stories, but surprisingly few. Studies of Gothic novels abound, but the Gothic, as we shall see, is another matter. The modern ghostly tale is as much a reaction against the Gothic as an outgrowth of it. Despite endless (largely interchangeable) anthology introductions through the years, Lovecraft's essay remains the most empathetic and original study of the genre to date. E. F. Bleiler is quite right in calling it "the finest historical discussion of supernatural fiction."[10] It is not so much a critical essay as a collection of chronologically arranged reminiscences of Lovecraft's favorite (and not so favorite) tales. Lovecraft, who was naturally very fond of horror stories, had read widely and manages to cram an extraordinary amount of information and opinion into sixty-six pages. He covers the majority of writers (from all periods) in a sentence or two, so that the work reads like an annotated bibliography. The annotation is, to say the least, unorthodox. Lovecraft's chronic addiction to hyperbole is as much in evidence here as in his fiction, but is not as debilitating. Indeed the style makes the book a great deal of fun. His description of M. R. James's ghosts is typical: "In inventing a new type of ghost, he has departed considerably from the conventional Gothic tradition; for where the older stock ghosts were pale and stately, and apprehended chiefly through the sense of sight, the average James ghost is lean, dwarfish, and hairy—a sluggish, hellish night-abomination midway betwixt beast and man—and usually *touched* before it is *seen*. Sometimes the spectre is of still more eccentric composition; a roll of flannel with spidery eyes, or an invisible entity which moulds itself in bedding and shows a *face of crumpled linen*."[11] There is clearly more of Lovecraft than of James in this italicized hysteria. Although Lovecraft appears to be warming up for a tale of his own, he nevertheless manages to make the important contrast between the impotence of the largely decorative Gothic ghosts and the more actively loathsome, menacing quality of modern ghosts.[12]

Lovecraft's is not a Freudian study, and I should make it clear that this one is not either. While it is true that repressed or displaced sexuality functions as an element in some of these stories (especially in stories which feature vampires on the make), it is not necessarily true that this is the dominant or most arresting element. (Since Freud's theories purport to explain human behavior, *any* story is theoretically a Freudian story.) Natural explanations to supernatural tales are almost always a depressing let-down and Freudian explanations particularly so. To reduce the stories to case studies is to rob them of their charm and power. The best Freudian study is "The Uncanny," by Freud himself, since it is enlivened by Freud's obvious respect for and enjoyment of the genre.

As for whom to discuss, I find myself in the classic dilemma of the anthology editors, that of having to justify omissions and slightings. From the many possibilities, this study will focus on three writers: Sheridan Le Fanu, M. R. James, and Algernon Blackwood. I have chosen these both for their quality and for their representative embodiment of patterns and boundaries. The study begins with a chapter devoted entirely to Le Fanu's "Green Tea," a tale which represents supernatural horror in its purest and most revolutionary manifestation. I have also included a separate chapter surveying the more refined horrors of the M. R. James antiquarian school.

Since this study is frankly biased in favor of writers who have received little attention, I am devoting relatively little space to Henry James. A massive number of articles have already been churned out in the "controversy" over whether the governess in *The Turn of the Screw* sees ghosts or hallucinates ghosts because she longs to bed down her employer. We need not add fuel to that feeble but unquenchable fire. The most sensible and moving commentary on this intractably enigmatic tale is provided by Virginia Woolf: her perception of the great absences and "silences" in the work say more about its essence than all the "proofs" and counterproofs set off by Edmund Wilson's early Freudian manifesto.[13] James's other ghostly tales have also received critical attention, especially "The Jolly Corner." And Leon Edel has provided exhaustive critical and historical commentary on all of James's ghostly tales.[14]

Edel's tendency to overpraise James is endemic of the exaggerated quality of what little commentary exists on the ghost story. The battle lines have always been drawn quickly and sharply; commentators usually deliver either unqualified raves or unqualified jeers. Peter Penzoldt proclaims that supernatural stories are the products of "the greatest masters of all times . . . Their writings are among the finest and most profound in modern literature." "Thus," he assures us, "the reader must not consider his love for weird fiction a vice."[15] Actually, as Hartley points out, it may well be a vice, or at least "slightly abnormal,"[16] and all the more pleasurable for being so. The negative side is typified by Samuel Hynes who (sounding more like T. S. Eliot than Eliot) dismisses the entire genre because it lacks "dogma": "If you remove doctrine and dogma from the religious instinct, what you have left is a debased or sentimentalized supernaturalism, things that go bump in the night, and that is, on the whole, what this strain of writing amounts to: of all the examples that one could cite, only 'The Turn of the Screw' is a substantial work of art."[17] "Substantial" is of course not defined. What is most revealing is that Hynes does not cite any of James's other ghostly tales, several of which are "substantial" in any meaningful sense of the term. (Critics are often unaware that James wrote others: Stern, for example, speaks of "Henry James' single and superlatively successful essay into the field, 'The Turn of the Screw.' "[18] This statement will come as some surprise to anyone who has read Edel's four-hundred-page collection.) Perhaps the most amusing diatribe is Edmund Wilson's famous attack on Lovecraft: "The only real horror in these fictions is the horror of bad taste and bad art."[19] Although they have been counter-attacking Wilson for the past thirty years, Lovecraft's fans have never been able to undo the damage caused by that wonderful sentence. (Wilson is actually easier on horror stories than on detective stories: he at least likes Poe and de la Mare, but dismisses all detective stories as "rubbish.") While these superlatives and denunciations are entertaining, they sometimes prevent the reader from assessing the distinctive strengths and flaws of writers who are neither as exalted nor worthless as critics insist.

In making selective judgments, my assumption is that a ghost story, like any story, is only as good as the author's prose style. Lovecraft is right when he maintains that "atmosphere is the all-important thing"[20] in the tale of terror: a compelling atmosphere can make us forget or overlook the banalities inherent in the genre. Atmosphere, however, is a function of style. Getting the atmosphere right takes considerable stylistic deftness, especially when the writer is trying for something more subtle than a stereotypical "Gothic" mood. Eschewing Gothic hyperbole, the best stories have elegant surfaces that gradually imply or reveal something not so elegant; the best chills are evoked with care and control.

Nevertheless, there is a popular mythology which insists that these stories are purely oral phenomena. According to this notion, the mere presence of the speaking voice displaces any need for form, structure, or verbal artistry. In Le Fanu's "Ultor de Lacy," the narrator speaks of his intention to recreate the aura and environment of the ghost story experience: "the old-fashioned parlour fireside and its listening circle of excited faces, and outside the wintry blast and moan of leafless boughs." He also complains of having to do this, stating that "the translation to cold type from oral narrative . . . is at best a trying one."[21] Basil Davenport, in his essay "On Telling Stories" carries this oral bias to its furthest extreme. "A story told even passably" (presumably with a different wording in any given telling), says Davenport, "is incomparably more effective than the same story read in solitude."[22] Is it true that the natural directness of the speaking voice counts for "incomparably" more than the admittedly prearranged, artificial techniques of metaphor, understatement, ambiguity, and irony? In confronting this question, I will also suggest a final compromise between hearing a story and reading it.

In using "ghost story" as a catch-all term, I am also compromising. All of these stories are apparitional, in one sense or another, and "ghost story" is as good a term as any. "Horror story" is not quite as all-inclusive and will be used more selectively. E. G. Swain, for example, keeps physical mayhem and revulsion out of his stories; he is strictly a "ghost story" writer and can be called a "horror story" writer only be stretching the term beyond comprehensible limits. There is little to be gained, however, by attempting to determine precisely what those limits are. It is enough to assume that a story like M. R. James's "Count Magnus" is both a ghost and horror story, for its ghosts do extremely nasty things to people. Most English tales fall into this class, and for them the terms can be used almost interchangeably. (Lovecraft's "supernatural horror" neatly fuses both terms.) Robert Aickman, one of the most skillful contemporary writers of supernatural tales, points out that even stories where we never see a ghost are still ghost stories: "A better title for the genre might be found, but the absence of the ghost seldom dispels the alarm. It can be almost worse if *someone else* apprehends the ghost, as in 'Seaton's Aunt'; or if you cannot tell whether it is a ghost or not, as in 'The Trains.' "[23]

Finding the appropriate language and tone for discussing this fiction is tricky business. Like the music of Poulenc or the films of Arthur Penn, it lies in a strange intermediary class between "popular" and "serious" art. Although grounded in the sensational and the outrageous, the better stories have larger reverberations (almost in spite of themselves) and frequently return to haunt our minds and sensibilities.

Part of their power can be attributed to a surprisingly large amount of ironic humor, an element which complicates their tone and increases their pungency. The most fascinating and adventurous attempt to classify this literature is Dorothy L. Sayers's in her *Third Omnibus of Crime* (a collection which is actually more an omnibus of ghostly stories than crime stories). Since she is a famous ratiocination fan, we would expect her to place more value on the detective story. Instead, using De Quincey's formulation, she assigns detective stories to the "literature of knowledge" and ghost stories to the "literature of power." With this distinction, we can expect detective stories to merely teach (as would a cook book) and ghost stories to move the soul by evoking the unteachable and unknowable:

> The horror-story (as opposed to the detective story) cares little for details of chemical composition. "Here," it says, "is a body that is, or was, the dwelling-place of a soul. It was haunted when it was alive by strange lusts, and fears and cruelties, and when it is destroyed it is not finished with. Its power has still to be made manifest. 'O Julius Caesar, thou art mighty yet!—Thy spirit walks abroad.' " It matters little whether we think of that power as a visible ghost or as a strange vindictive corruption fastening upon the murderer's heart. That is a matter for the writer's taste and fancy. But the dead will show their might, in some fashion or another—*though how, we do not know*.
>   "We know well enough," replies the detective story, "The murderer will be detected and hanged, and there will be an end of it."
>   "An end of it?" says the story of horror. "You will add corpse to corpse—and what then?"[24]

Rarely is there "an end of it" in these tales. After the book is closed, the deadly apparition is still at large, both in the story and in the reader's mind.

CHAPTER I

"GREEN TEA":
THE ARCHETYPAL GHOST STORY

In 1839, a new kind of ghost appeard in English fiction. The appearance, in Joseph Sheridan Le Fanu's "Schalken the Painter," went unnoticed, for Le Fanu was an unknown, and his tales were published anonymously. By a strange coincidence, "The Fall of the House of Usher" came out the same year, but Poe's more celebrated tale is a landmark of a different order, an exercise in cosmic paranoia rather than a tale of the supernatural. Le Fanu's creations were real ghosts who stubbornly refused to confine themselves to the shabby psyches of aristocratic neurotics, yet somehow managed to emerge from within as well as invade from without; who (unlike Mrs. Radcliffe's ghosts) could not be explained away, yet who would have nothing to do with what Oliver Onions once called "the groans and clankings of the grosser spook."[1] "Schalken the Painter" was as revolutionary in execution as in the peculiar nature of its two ghosts. The story tells of the abduction, rape, and final seduction of a young woman by a living corpse, all from the point of view of the girl's befuddled uncle and horrified fiance. Le Fanu handled both the necrophilia and the supernaturalism in the tale with a new anti-Gothic restraint. As if reluctant to reveal its sordid and marvelous secrets, the plot develops itself entirely through suggestion and indirection, building toward an extraordinary dream sequence involving the transformation of a coffin into a Victorian four-poster bed. It is a chilling performance.

Yet "Schalken the Painter" is not the most refined or the

most representative of Le Fanu's tales. It is rather the promising start of a long, influential career in ghostly fiction. The culmination of that career is "Green Tea," a late tale which represents the new ghost story in its most uncompromising form. "Green Tea," the story of a man who literally has a monkey on his back, can serve as an ideal introduction not only to Le Fanu's other tales, but to the entire ghostly school that he spawned. It is a thoroughly modern tale, and its modernity, so unexpectedly daring, is the key to understanding the contradictions between plot and theme in more ambivalent tales such as "The Mysterious Lodger" and "The Familiar."

Le Fanu first published "Green Tea" in Dickens's magazine *All the Year Round* (1869) and later reprinted it in *In A Glass Darkly* (1872), a remarkable collection of his late tales which includes "Mr. Justice Harbottle," "The Familiar," "Carmilla," and (somewhat inappropriately since there is no supernatural episode) "The Room in the Dragon Volant." With the possible exception of "Carmilla," no other Le Fanu tale has been so widely discussed. Its visibility, so unusual for Le Fanu, can probably be accounted for by its novel concept. V. S. Pritchett, Edna Kenton, William Buckler, Nelson Browne, and E. F. Benson have all sung the praises of Le Fanu's demonic monkey.[2] Speaking for all of them, Buckler states that "Green Tea" "is generally given first place in the canon of his work," while Pritchett extends the generalization by calling it one of "the best half-dozen ghost stories in the English language."

The structure of "Green Tea" is a perfect illustration of M. R. James's model for the modern ghost story:

> Let us, then, be introduced to the actors in a placid way; let us see them going about their ordinary business, undisturbed by forebodings, pleased with their surroundings; and into this calm environment let the ominous thing put out its head, unobtrusively at first, and then more insistently, until it holds the stage.[3]

Le Fanu was the first to use this strategy, and he applies it with particular deftness here. The victim in "Green Tea," the Reverend Mr. Jennings, is introduced to the reader by the central narrator, Dr. Martin Hesselius, who in the course of the tale becomes Jennings's therapist. We first see Jennings at a congenial, tedious dinner party, conversing with Hesselius. They are discussing a German first edition of Hesselius's "Essays on Metaphysical Medicine." The conversation is learned but also abstracted and rather silly. Only one sentence appears to have any relevance to a possible ghostly experience: it is a hint involving the motivations for Jennings's odd curiosity concerning Hesselius's exotic research: "I suppose [says Hesselius] you have been turning the subject over again in your mind, or something has happened lately to revive your interest in it."[4]

The conversation, with its pedantry and innuendo, is a prefiguration of M. R. James's dialogue, as are the clues which reinforce its implications. Something indeed "has happened." Although Jennings is a reserved, "perfectly gentleman like man," he has a few revealing quirks. For one thing, he has a peculiar tendency to flee from the pulpit during his own sermons: "After proceeding a certain way in the service, he has on a sudden stopped short, and after a silence, apparently quite unable to resume, he has fallen into solitary, inaudible prayer, his hands and eyes uplifted and then pale as death, and in the agitation of a strange shame and horror, descended trembling, and got into the vestry-room, leaving his congregation, without explanation, to themselves" (180). The situation becomes so critical that Jennings resorts to having an alternate clergyman waiting in the wings "should he become thus suddenly incapacitated." Hesselius also notices a "certain oddity" in Jennings's dinner conversation: "Mr. Jennings has a way of looking sideways upon the carpet, as if his eye followed the movements of something there" (180). The final oddity is revealed by the hostess, Lady Mary Heyduke, when she remarks that she used to quarrel with Jennings over his addiction to green tea. Hesselius agrees that Jennings was once "extravagantly" addicted to the stuff, but insists that "he has quite given that up" (183).

Le Fanu, a careful artist, was undoubtedly aware of the ludicrousness of all this. The notion that humor is anathema to horror is one of the persistent cliches of anthology introduc-

tions. It is also one of the most erroneous, as anyone who has
read Bierce or Hartley can attest. Humor, particularly when
ironic or absurd, is inextricably fused with supernatural
horror in fiction. I have found the linkage to be consistent
throughout the field: the reader automatically integrates the
two elements as he reads. In "Green Tea," the first apparition scene skirts the same arbitrary borderline between the
laughable and the horrible as the clues which anticipate it.
The absurdity of the premise—the lethal apparition is, after all,
a monkey—weakens the impact not at all; indeed the strange
power of the tale lies in the irony that something intrinsically
ridiculous can drive a man to destroy himself.

Jennings, of course, is not amused by this creature. His
account of the first apparition is peculiarly unnerving and
deserves to be quoted at length as a paradigm of Le Fanu's
apparition scenes:

"The interior of the omnibus was nearly dark. I had observed in the
corner opposite to me at the other side, and at the end next the
horses, two small circular reflections, as it seemed to me of a reddish
light. They were about two inches apart, and about the size of those
small brass buttons that yachting men used to put upon their jackets.
I began to speculate, as listless men will, upon this trifle, as it seemed.
From what centre did that faint but deep red light come, and from
what—glass beads, buttons, toy decorations—was it reflected? We
were lumbering along gently, having nearly a mile still to go. I had
not solved the puzzle, and it became in another minute more odd, for
these two luminous points, with a sudden jerk, descended nearer and
nearer the floor, keeping still their relative distance and horizontal
position, and then, as suddenly, they rose to the level of the seat on
which I was sitting and I saw them no more.

"My curiosity was now really excited and before I had time to
think, I saw again these two dull lamps, again together near the
floor; again they disappeared, and again in their old corner I saw
them.

"So, keeping my eyes upon them, I edged quietly up my own side,
towards the end at which I still saw these tiny discs of red.

"There was very little light in the 'bus. It was nearly dark. I leaned
forward to aid my endeavour to discover what these little circles
really were. They shifted position a little as I did so. I began now to
perceive an outline of something black, and I soon saw, with tolerable
distinctness, the outline of a small black monkey, pushing its face forward in mimicry to meet mine; those were its eyes, and I now dimly
saw its teeth grinning at me.

"I drew back not knowing whether it might not meditate a spring.

I fancied that one of the passengers had forgot this ugly pet, and wishing to ascertain something of its temper, though not caring to trust my fingers to it, I poked my umbrella softly towards it. It remained immovable—up to it—*through* it. For through it, and back and forward it passed, without the slightest resistance.

"I can't in the least, convey to you the kind of horror that I felt." (193-194)

Throughout this passage, the emphasis is on the way Jennings perceives the apparition rather than on the apparition itself. Jennings's reaction is the important thing, as is the reader's: we are forced to see this strange abomination exactly as Jennings sees it. It scarcely matters whether the thing is "real" or hallucinated; in a good horror tale this distinction is effaced. Supernatural horror in fiction has little to do with the materiality or immateriality of spooks. What counts is the authenticity of the experience. The scene works because of the intricate perspectival character of the writing, a technique which anticipates Henry James's *The Turn of the Screw* and "Sir Edmund Orme." The most remarkable aspect of Le Fanu's perspectivism is his use of synecdoche, a poetic mechanism which allows him to straddle the boundary between the explicit and the indirect. His use of the device is more radical in other tales, notably "The Haunting of the Tiled House" in which the unearthly force is represented solely by a disembodied hand. Here we visualize the creature in terms of its eyes, although "these two dull lamps" dimly illuminate the rest of the shape.

Jennings stumbles from the omnibus "in a panic," discovering to his "indescribable relief" that the thing is gone. Like all of Le Fanu's victims, he convinces himself that it was all a fleeting "illusion." But on the way home he looks up "with loathing and horror" to see it creeping along beside him on a brick wall. From this point on, the creature persecutes Jennings with incredible tenacity. As in the first apparition scene, the sufferer's emotions are communicated consistently through his reaction to the demon's eyes. During the initial phase of the persecution, the eyes are "dazed and languid," "jaded and sulkey," "sullen and sick." Yet they have "unfathomable malignanty" and above all, "intense vigilance." "In all situations, at all hours," says the unfortunate Jennings, "it is awake and looking at me; that never changes"(196).

Thus begins this extraordinary obsession, chronicled in graded steps: three "stages" in a hellish "journey." In the "Second Stage," the demon mysteriously disappears for a month, during which time Jennings again experiences an illusory respite. But then it returns with "new energy," "brooding over some atrocious plan." This phase of the persecution is characterized by many such disappearances: "it has sometimes been away so long as nearly two months, once for three," Jennings tells his therapist. "Its absence always exceeds a fortnight, although it may be but by a single day. Fifteen days having past since I saw it last, it may return now at any moment"(197). At once arbitrary and mysteriously calculated, this time span induces the maximum amount of anxiety, causing the patient to look progressively "like death." It is a typically cruel touch, which Le Fanu is fond of using in situations of otherworldly harrassment (c.f "The Familiar"). Another painful characteristic of the second phase is Jennings's new inability to attain relief by simply shutting his eyes: "I know it is not to be accounted for physically, but I do actually see it though my eyes are closed" (199). As part of its new militancy, the creature will "squat" in Jennings's prayer book during holy services, obscuring any passage he attempts to read his congregation. It is presumably during these occasions that Jennings flees from the pulpit.

In the third and final stage, the demon "speaks" to Jennings. Unlike Gothic writers, with their fatal predilection for chatty spectres, Le Fanu shrewdly avoids any attempt to reproduce its actual words.[5] Instead, he allows Jennings to suggest the sound metaphorically, through a kind of ghostly music: "It is not by my ears it reaches me—it comes like a singing through my head"(200). Although Jennings never quotes the lyrics of this "song," he lets us know that they are thoroughly unpleasant, particularly during his abortive attempts at prayer:

> "This faculty, the power of speaking to me, will be my undoing. It won't let me pray, it interrupts me with dreadful blasphemies. I dare

not go on, I could not. Oh! Doctor, can the skill and thought, and prayers of man avail me nothing!" (200)

They indeed avail him nothing. In these tales, prayer is utterly ineffectual—as are faith and good works. Like most Le Fanu, "Green Tea" does not end happily. In the final phase, the demon tries to persuade his victim to commit suicide. Jennings, who after three years of demonic persecution does not need much persuading, ends his "journey" by cutting his throat. Suicide is the only way out for him, and he is unique among Le Fanu's victims in perceiving this. As in Greek tragedy, the final horror is not rendered directly but is reported by a messenger, in this case Jennings's servant. As always, Le Fanu avoids being too direct: he leaves the awful details to the reader's imagination, yet still gets in a good bloody scene by having Hesselius clinically inspect the "immense pool of blood on the floor" of Jennings's "sombre and now terrible room" (204).

"Green Tea" is every bit as twisted, disturbing and unresolvable as it seems. Nevertheless, by imposing orthodox explanations and theoretical systems on the story, critics have done what they could to dissipate its mystery and menace. The orthodoxies divide into two camps, the Freudian and the Christian, each of which has a predictable explanation for Jennings's persecution. To Peter Penzoldt, Jennings's monkey is simply "the product of schizoid neurosis"; to V. S. Pritchett, it is "dark and hairy with original sin," and its persecutions symbolize "justified" retribution for specific sins; to Michael Begnal, the monkey is sent to punish a clergyman who has "lost his faith" and whose "intellectual pride" has "cut him off from God."[6]

The problem with such theories is that they convert possibilities into solutions. M. R. James, who modelled his stories after Le Fanu's, once stated, "It is not amiss sometimes to leave a loophole for a natural explanation, but I would say, let the loophole be so narrow as not to be quite practicable."[14] This teasing, enigmatic quality, so obvious to any writer in the genre, is missed by theory-obsessed critics. In "Green Tea," the Freudian "loophole" is narrow indeed. We are not given enough information about the near-anonymous Jennings to conclude that he is "schizoid" or "sexually repressed." We are told only that he is shy and unassuming.

The Christian interpretation is even flimsier. There is no doubt that Jennings's obsession is somehow connected with an intense, unspeakable feeling of guilt. The text contains many references to this feeling: he collapses from the altar "in the agitation of a strange shame and horror"(180); he looks at Hesselius "guiltily" during their first conversation (182); he even cries "God forgive me!" during a later conversation (192). What the text does not tell us is what Jennings needs to be forgiven for, what crime he has committed to merit such a hideous, ultimately lethal punishment. As we shall see, the only character who could conceivably be accused of "intellectual pride" is Dr. Hesselius. Indeed, if we assume with Begnal that Jennings committed a mortal sin by researching the non-Christian religious beliefs of the ancients, we must ask why Hesselius is not also pursued to the grave by the avenging monkey, for he is guilty of the same heterodox research. Nor is there any evidence that Jennings has lost his faith; on the contrary, he is a pious, devout Christian who ceases to pray only when the monkey literally prevents him from doing so by shrieking blasphemies in his ear.

The truth is that Jennings has done nothing but drink green tea. The very title of the tale registers the fundamental irony: the awful disjuncture between cause and effect, crime and punishment. What emerges is an irrational, almost Kafkaesque feeling of guilt and persecution. Like Joseph K., Jennings is ceaselessly pursued and tormented for no discernible reason. A persistent experience in modern fiction is a situation in which the main character wakes up one morning on a tightrope and does not know how he got there. This is precisely the predicament Jennings finds himself in. Although S. M. Ellis calls Le Fanu a "tragic" writer,[7] "Green Tea" is closer to modern tragi-comedy. Jennings never experiences even a flash of tragic recognition; on the contrary, he never knows why this horrible thing is happening. There is no insight, no justice and therefore no tragedy. There is only absurd cruelty, a grim world view which endures in the reader's mind long after the hairs have settled on the back of the neck.

Though ultimately deterministic, this world view is not based on a coherent or knowable determinism—there is neither the benign workings of Providence nor the naturalism of Zola or Dreiser. The sense of doom in these stories emanates from a uniquely hostile cosmos vaguely suggestive of the purblind doomsters which later pursue Thomas Hardy's characters. But Le Fanu is not interested in programmatic philosophical consistency. In trying to get at the source of the horror, various characters suggest various possibilities—all of them bleak—yet final solutions elude them, as they elude the reader. One event leads inexorably to another once the pursuit begins, but the reason behind it is known only to the otherworldly invaders. Causality is present, but Le Fanu's victims experience only Crass Causality, blind and mechanical, yet efficiently murderous once the cosmos gives someone a bad throw of the dice. Jennings dimly perceives the magnitude of the forces massed against him in one of his final, most pathetic speeches:

> But as food is taken in softly at the lips, and then brought under the teeth, as the tip of the little finger caught in a mill crank will draw in the hand, and the arm, and the whole body, so the miserable mortal who has been once caught firmly by the end of the finest fibre of his nerve, is drawn in and in, by the enormous machinery of hell, until he is as I am. Yes, Doctor, as *I* am, for a while I talk to you, and implore relief, I feel that my prayer is for the impossible, and my pleading with the inexorable. (200)

Jennings is horribly right in his perception that the workings of the grisly machinery are "inexorable" and that his "prayer is for the impossible."

Despite the resemblance of all this to Hap in its most perverse manipulations, there is an ominous point at which the analogy breaks down. Once Le Fanu's hellish machine begins grinding, it does so with Hardyesque remorselessness, but also with a strange awareness of purpose which goes beyond the half-consciousness of the Immanent Will. If Hardy's cosmos is struggling to attain consciousness, Le Fanu's has already attained it, or is at least well along the way. If there is no benevolent or rational purpose behind things, there does seem to be a sinister purpose. James Barton, another Le Fanu victim, speaks of this conspiracy in Manichaean terms in "The

Familiar." Jennings, lacking even tentative answers, is obsessed with "machinery" and process, with the "stages" of his torment:

> "In the dark, as you shall presently hear, there are peculiarities. It is
> a small monkey, perfectly black. It had only one peculiarity—a char-
> acter of malignity—unfathomable malignity. During the first year it
> looked sullen and sick. But this character of intense malice and vigi-
> lance was always underlying that surly languor. During all that
> time it acted as if on a plan of giving me as little trouble as was
> consistent with watching me. Its eyes were never off me. I have never
> lost sight of it, except in my sleep, light or dark, day or night, since
> it came here excepting when it withdraws for some weeks at a time,
> unaccountably.
> "In total dark it is visible as in daylight. I do not mean merely its
> eyes. It is *all* visible distinctly in a halo that resembles a glow of red
> embers and which accompanies it in all its movements.
> "When it leaves me for a time, it is always at night, in the dark,
> and in the same way. It grows at first uneasy, and then furious, and
> then advances towards me, grinning and shaking, its paws clenched,
> and, at the same time, there comes the appearance of fire in the
> grate. I never have any fire. I can't sleep in the room where there is
> any, and it draws nearer and nearer to the chimney, quivering, it
> seems, with rage, and when its fury rises to the highest pitch, it
> springs into the grate, and up the chimney, and I see it no more.
> "When first this happened, I thought I was released. I was now a
> new man. A day passed—a night—and no return, and a blessed
> week—a week—another week. I was always on my knees, Dr. Hessel-
> ius, always thanking God and praying. A whole month passed of li-
> berty, but on a sudden, it was with me again. . . .
> "It was with me, and the malice which before was torpid under a
> sullen exterior, was now active. It was perfectly unchanged in every
> other respect. This new energy was apparent in its activity and its
> looks, and soon in other ways.
> "For a time, you will understand, the change was shown only in an
> increased vivacity, and an air of menace, as if it were always brooding
> over some atrocious plan. It eyes, as before, were never off me."
> (196-197)

The victim of "an atrocious plan," intricately conceived and
faultlessly executed, Jennings is denied even an inkling of the
ultimate purpose behind that plan.

In this sense, Jennings is in a bleaker predicament than
Poe's Roderick Usher, who is powerless largely because he
thinks he is. Usher's main problem seems to be a kind of
self-inflicted catatonia: since the horrors in Poe's tale are

completely localized in a single house, they would presumably
lessen if Usher would take the narrator's advice and go somewhere else; but the famous twist is that the house cannot be
separated from Usher's mind, as Usher himself reveals to us
in his allegorical poem and in his abstract paintings of subterranean tunnels.[8] More than anything else, Usher needs a
therapist. But Jennings, who has a therapist, is entirely helpless, for the horror which pursues him is more than a psychological phenomenon. Therapy does him no good; he is victimized by something finally independent of his psyche. In
the passage describing the monkey's leap up the chimney,
Le Fanu is careful to depict a fiend who is extraordinarily
alive, the active incarnation of some unrelenting principle
of hatred. The symbiotic connection between setting and
psyche, so important in "The Fall of the House of Usher"
and "M. S. Found In A Bottle," does not apply here. Le Fanu's
settings are often evocative in themselves (see "Sir Dominick's Bargain"), but they are irrelevant to the main action:
his doomed heroes are pursued wherever they go, are tormented in the most unlikely places; their ghostly tormenters
see no need to confine themselves in depressing Gothic
houses and are likely to appear anywhere, often in broad
daylight. (In "The Familiar," James Barton is chased by the
Watcher, a spectre who is fond of appearing not only in daylight, but in crowds; nor does he mind traveling long distances when Barton tries to skip the country.)

This is not to say that Le Fanu is unconcerned with psychology. On the contrary, his tales deal repeatedly with dark
states of consciousness. The difference between "Green Tea"
and Edmund Wilson's version of *The Turn of the Screw* is
that this inner darkness is a sinisterly accurate measure of
the outer world rather than a neurotic projection. Like the
madness of Lear, the derangement of Jennings's mind is a
mirror image of a derangement in the cosmos, although
Jennings has neither the insight nor the catharsis of Lear.
That the infernal region in Jennings's psyche reflects not only
reality, but the fundamental reality, is hinted at in a passage
in Swedenborg's "Arcana Celestia," which Hesselius trans-
lated from the Latin:

"When man's interior sight is opened, which is that of
his spirit, then there appear the things of another life, which cannot
possibly be made visible to the bodily sight." . . . .

"By the internal sight it has been granted me to see the things that
are in the other life, more clearly than I see those that are in the
world. From these considerations, it is evident that external vision
exists from interior vision, and this from a vision still more interior,
and so on." . . . .

"If evil spirits could perceive that they were associated with man,
and yet that they were spirits separate from him, and if they could
flow in into the things of his body, they would attempt by a thousand
means to destroy him; for they hate man with a deadly hatred." . . . .
(186)

Placing the passage in context with Jennings's experience, it
becomes apparent that the doors of perception open straight
into hell; they are kept mercifully shut for the most part, but
can be flung open by the most absurdly inadvertent act, in
this case by the drinking of green tea.

It is just as well that little has been made of Le Fanu's
connection with Swedenborg,[9] for Le Fanu's version represents a distortion, or at least a darkening of the original. The
passage which Hesselius translates goes on to say that the
"wicked genii" do not attack those who are "in the good of
faith." The Christian is "continually protected by the lord."
But this protection does not work for Jennings (who writes
"Deus misereatur mei" in the margin of the Swedenborg
text). Without the saving light of a benevolent deity, Le Fanu's
mystical psychology is far more malevolent than Swedenborg's: what we have in this psychological landscape are
increasingly deeper layers of consciousness, each one increasingly diabolical—an infinite darkness.

The darkness in Le Fanu is quite different from the "blackness of darkness"[10] in Poe or the "great power of blackness"
Melville found in Hawthorne. In Poe, darkness is a thick,
palpable texture, opaque and impenetrable, which permeates
mind and matter like an endless sewage. In Hawthorne,
darkness is a moral quality deriving from the traditional symbolic equation of darkness with evil. Both writers paint with
a wide brush, darkening their prose immediately with adjectives like "gloomy" and "inscrutable." Though brilliantly
evoked, theirs is often a melodramatic world where colors

have allegorical rigidity. In Le Fanu, where the fiend is as likely to appear in the full light of the Sunday church service as in the gloom of a mouldering house, where he is comfortable squatting in the prayerbook rather than seething in the sinner's bosom, colors are used sparingly, sometimes monochromatically. Much of the traditional color symbolism remains: the blacks and reds often suggest as much evil and violence as they do in *Macbeth*; the lurid halo emanating from the monkey like "a glow of red embers" gives off the same satanic light as Ethan Brand's lime kiln.

For the most part, however, Le Fanu's colors elude allegorical equations. Unfettered by an orderly moral universe, they have a half-tinted quality which is somehow more unsettling than the extravagant darkness and storminess of the Gothic writers:

> The sun had already set, and the red reflected light of the western sky illuminated the scene with the peculiar effect with which we are all familiar. The hall seemed very dark, but, getting to the back drawingroom, whose windows command the west, I was again in the same dusky light.
>
> I sat down, looking out upon the richly-wooded landscape that glowed in the grand and melancholy light which was every moment fading. The corners of the room were already dark; all was growing dim, and the gloom was insensibly toning my mind, already prepared for what was sinister. I was waiting alone for his arrival, which soon took place. The door communicating with the front room opened, and the tall figure of Mr. Jennings, faintly seen in the ruddy twilight, came, with quiet stealthy steps, into the room.
>
> We shook hands, and taking a chair to the window, where there was still light enough to enable us to see each other's faces, he sat down beside me, and, placing his hand upon my arm, with scarcely a word of preface began his narrative. . . .
>
> The faint glow of the west, the pomp of the then lonely woods of Richmond, were before us, behind and about us the darkening room, and on the stony face of the sufferer—for the character of his face, though still gentle and sweet, was changed—rested that dim, odd glow which seems to descend and produce, where it touches, lights, sudden though faint, which are lost almost without gradation, in darkness. The silence, too, was utter: not a distant wheel, or bark, or whistle from without; and within the depressing stillness of an invalid bachelor's house." (191)

What do we make of this strange twilight, dim and translucent one minute, "grand and melancholy" the next; "every moment fading," yet reappearing suddenly, only to be "lost, almost without gradation, in darkness"? The passage seems naturalistic enough, at least up to a point (The sunset has "the peculiar effect with which we are all familiar.") Yet the lights and shadows become so blurred and undefined as to become almost interchangeable. Faint points of light seem to go on and off like stars suddenly going out and reappearing in a cloudy sky. In the next to last sentence, with its twisted, almost Jamesian syntax, this "odd glow" is associated with Jennings's face. The "almost" here suggests a subtle gradation, a hierarchy of twilight worlds, each of which gives off its own unearthly lights, swallowing them up again almost instantly.

Jennings has accidentally summoned a creature from one of these worlds, and his face shows the price he has paid: it has assumed the same deathlike appearance as Jennings's new companion; it even emits the same strange lights. Le Fanu's imagery suggests the shifting, dissolving colors of a nightmare. Ambiguous and undefined, his colors are like those in our dreams, much harder to recall than the technicolor images of Poe or Monk Lewis.

The reader can experience the relief of waking, simply by closing the book and turning on every light in the house. The doomed protagonists are not so fortunate. In Jennings's case, his demise seems to be hastened by the incompetence of his therapist. Hesselius deserves close examination, for he appears to be the first psychiatrist in English literature. Since he is pre-Freudian by at least thirty years, he has a hard time defining just what he is, calling himself at various times a medical philosopher, a philosophical physician and even a doctor of Metaphysical Medicine. He is distinctly a therapist, however, claiming to have diagnosed "two hundred and thirty cases more or less nearly akin to that I have entitled 'Green Tea.' "(208). This is a staggering thought, suggesting that Hesselius has dealt with a large number of what are surely the most bizarre patients in the annals of psychiatry. If the prefaces to the *In A Glass Darkly* are to be taken seriously, he has had to confront such things as living corpses, demonic monkeys, and lesbian vampires.[12]

All this has been hard on him, as his ineptness in treating Jennings all too clearly reveals. After Jennings unfolds his tale, Hesselius is at an obvious loss as to what to do. At one particularly strained point, immediately following the oration on "the enormous machinery of hell," Hesselius can only say: "I endeavored to calm his visibly increasing agitation and told him that he must not despair"(200). This is fatuous advice: there is every reason to despair, especially in the absence of any concrete suggestions. Following Jennings's depressing account of a near-suicide attempt, Hesselius's advice is even worse:

> "Yes, yes; it is always urging me to crimes, to injure others, or myself. You see, Doctor, the situation is urgent, it is indeed. When I was in Shropshire, a few weeks, ago" (Mr. Jennings was speaking rapidly and trembling now, holding my arm with one hand, and looking in my face), "I went out one day with a party of friends for a walk: my persecutor, I tell you, was with me at the time. I lagged behind the rest: the country near the Dee, you know, is beautiful. Our path happened to lie near a coal mine, and at the verge of the wood is a perpendicular shaft, they say, a hundred and fifty feet deep. My niece had remained behind with me—she knows, of course, nothing of the nature of my sufferings. She knew, however, that I had been ill, and was low, and she remained to prevent my being quite alone. As we loitered slowly on together, the brute that accompanied me was urging me to throw myself down the shaft. I tell you now—oh, sir, think of it!—the one consideration that saved me from that hideous death was the fear lest the shock of witnessing the occurrence should be too much for the poor girl. I asked her to go on and walk with her friends, saying that I could go no further. She made excuses, and the more I urged her the firmer she became. She looked doubtful and frightened. I suppose there was something in my looks or manner that alarmed her; but she would not go, and that literally saved me. You had no idea, sir, that a living man could be made so abject a slave of Satan," he said with a ghastly groan and a shudder.
> There was a pause here, and I said, "You *were* preserved nevertheless. It was the act of God. You are in his hands, and in the power of no other being: be confident therefore for the future." (201)

Jennings's concern for the little girl's reaction, even at the climax of his own suicidal despair, strengthens our feeling that he is a scrupulously sensitive, compassionate man, undeserving of this torment. But the passage is more revealing of Hesselius. "You see, doctor, the situation is urgent, it is indeed" is a chilling understatement, yet all the philosophic physician can do is offer platitudes—the solace of a deity who is either indifferent or as impotent as Hesselius himself. This advice is more than merely unctuous and ineffectual: the claim that Jennings is "in the power of no other being" is demonstrably false.

Nor does his epilogue, "A Word for Those Who Suffer," do anything to enhance his professional credibility. This final chapter is in the form of a letter to Professor Van Loo of Leyden, a chemist who has suffered from Jennings's malady and whom Hesselius claims to have cured. It is a suspiciously self-serving document:

> Who, under God, cured you? Your humble servant, Martin Hesselius. Let me rather adopt the more emphasised piety of a certain good old French surgeon of three hundred years ago: "I treated, and God cured you."
>
> There is no one affliction of mortality more easily and certainly reducible, with a little patience, and a rational confidence in the physician. With these simple conditions, I look upon the cure as absolutely certain.
>
> You are to remember that I had not even commenced to treat Mr. Jennings' case. I have not any doubt that I should have cured him perfectly in eighteen months, or possibly it might have extended to two years. . . .
>
> You know my tract on "The Cardinal Functions of the Brain." I there, by the evidence of innumerable facts, prove, as I think, the high probability of a circulation arterial and venous in its mechanism, through the nerves. Of this system, thus considered, the brain is the heart. The fluid, which is propagated hence through one class of nerves, returns in an altered state through another, and the nature of that fluid is spiritual, though not immaterial, any more than, as I before remarked, light or electricity are so.
>
> By various abuses, among which the habitual use of such agents as green tea is one, this fluid may be affected as to its quality, but it is more frequently disturbed as to equilibrium. This fluid being that which we have in common with spirits, a congestion found upon the masses of brain or nerve, connected with the interior sense, forms a surface unduly exposed, on which disembodied spirits may operate: communication is thus more or less effectually established. Between this brain circulation and the heart circulation there is an intimate sympathy. The seat, or rather the instrument of exterior vision, is the eye. The seat of interior vision is the nervous tissue and brain, immediately about and above the eyebrow. You remember how effectually I dissipated your pictures by the simple application of iced eau-de-cologne. Few cases, however, can be treated exactly alike with anything like rapid success. Cold acts powerfully as a repellant of the nervous fluid. Long enough continued it will even produce that per-

manent insensibility which we call numbness, and a little longer muscular as well as sensational paralysis.

I have not, I repeat, the slightest doubt that I should have first dimmed and ultimately sealed that inner eye which Mr. Jennings had inadvertently opened. . . . It is by acting steadily upon the body, by a simple process, that this result is produced—and inevitably produced—I have never yet failed.

Poor Mr. Jennings made away with himself. But that catastrophe was the result of a totally different malady, which, as it were, projected itself upon the disease which was established. His case was in the distinctive manner a complication, and the complaint under which he really succumbed, was hereditary suicidal mania. Poor Mr. Jennings I cannot call a patient of mine, for I had not even begun to treat his case, and he had not yet given me, I am convinced, his full and unreserved confidence. If the patient do not array himself on the side of the disease, his cure is certain. (206-07)

The immediate point of interest here is the earnest but tortured attempt to reconcile medical science with mystical experience, a commonplace exercise in nineteenth and early twentieth-century weird fiction.[13] In relation to the story, however, the epilogue is not so earnest. It raises a variety of questions. Why did Hesselius not share any of these insights with his patient, a man on the verge of self-destruction? Why did he not tell him that his cure would be a "simple process"? Why did he not describe this process and thereby relieve Jennings's paranoia? Leaving aside the believability of this "absolutely certain" cure why did he not produce the magical "iced eau-de-cologne" and douse the wretched man with it? The final dismissal of Jennings's case as "hereditary suicidal mania," without any evidence, is an ugly rationalization. The wonder is that Jennings, unremittingly persecuted for three years, did not kill himself sooner; if anything, the evidence indicates an unusually strong psyche.

But the oddest thing about this addendum is its failure to explain its author's behaviour in the period between Jennings's narration and his suicide. After giving his account, Jennings understandably breaks down weeping (despite Hesselius's disingenuous "He seemed comforted"). Hesselius does have one concrete bit of comfort to offer: "One promise I exacted, which was that should the monkey return, I should be sent for immediately" (202). Taking his doctor at his word,

Jennings tries to contact Hesselius "immediately" after the
monkey's next appearance, which is predictably soon:

> Dear Dr. Hesselius—It is here. You had not been an hour gone when it
> returned. It is speaking. It knows all that has happened. It knows
> everything—it knows you, and is frantic and atrocious. It reviles. I send
> you this. It knows every word I have written—I write. This I promised
> and I therefore write, but I fear very confused, very' incoherently, I
> am so interrupted, disturbed.(203)

Hesselius, however, is not to be found. Intentionally making
his whereabouts unknown, he has fled when he is most need-
ed to an unknown address where he intends to dabble with
his metaphysical medicines "without the possibility of intrusion or distraction"(202). He seems to need therapy himself,
so shut off is he from the consequences of his actions. The
immediate consequence is that Jennings, feeling totally alone,
cuts his throat.

Hesselius is only marginally concerned with the well-being
of his patient. His chief motivation—which reaches a state of
frenzied anticipation—is his determination to validate his
theories. As the epilogue implies, he is less saddened than
annoyed by his patient's death; by that act, Jennings has
robbed him of his big chance.

We can reasonably conclude that Le Fanu did not mean us to
take this epilogue on the same level of seriousness as Hesselius assumes we do. His claims, accusations, and actions are
dubious enough in themselves; set against the powerful authenticity of Jennings's narrative, they make sense only as dramatic irony. Unless seen as ironic, the "Word for Those Who
Suffer" becomes an aesthetic blunder. There is nothing organic about this final chapter; it seems distinctly tacked on, a
needless diatribe which ruins the tale if taken at face value.
But seen as ironic, it underscores the hopelessness of Jennings's predicament.

As the less than reliable narrator of a horror tale, Hesselius is part of a tradition which begins with Poe's narrator
in "The Tell-Tale Heart" and culminates in the governess's
account in *The Turn of the Screw*. This is not to say that
Hesselius is a Gothic villain—a frothing madman or an osten-
tatiously evil doctor. Like everything else in the story, he is

difficult to pin down: earnest and well-meaning in the opening pages, he seems progressively more ineffectual, even
senile, at worst evincing a precarious ego which distorts his
judgement. In other respects as well, the narrative problems
are more complex than those in Poe. Hesselius is not the
only narrator of "Green Tea." The tale has a prologue as well
as a conclusion; as William Buckler has shown, the prologue
is also problematic:

> The story is filtered to the reader through three "carefully educated"
> men of science: the supposed editor, or "medical secretary"; Dr.
> Hesselius, the narrator; and Professor Van Loo, chemist and student
> of history, metaphysics, and medicine, to whom a correspondent
> would presumably write with conscientiousness. And yet each is a
> fallible authority: the editor is a confessed "enthusiast" who has taken
> Dr. Hesselius as his "master"; Dr. Hesselius, besides suffering from
> an acutely sensitive ego, obviously has no authority within the med-
> ical fraternity, is theoretical and categorical, and seems unduly intent
> upon rationalizing the perfect record of his "cures," and Dr. Van
> Loo, according to the narrator, has suffered from a similar "affec-
> tion," while, according to the editor, he is an "unlearned reader."[14]

Though accurate and concise as a summary, Buckler's introduction does not attempt to resolve the obvious question
it raises: why does Le Fanu bother with this narrative filtering device at all? This is a difficult question to answer, for
"Green Tea" is unlike other tales which saddle us with unreliable or multiple narrators: we get little sense of the moral
complexity found in Stevenson, the pathological involutions
found in Poe, or the fanatically refined sensibility found in
Henry James.

As an intentionally fuzzy narrative, "Green Tea" is similar to
several tales in Ambrose Bierce's *In the Midst of Life* and
Can Such Things Be? Like Bierce's "The Moonlit Road" and
"The Suitable Surroundings," "Green Tea" seems arbitrarily
burdened with narrators and editors.[15] Yet the seeming arbi-
trariness of the narrative scheme imparts a unique atmosphere
to these tales. Le Fanu anticipates Bierce in his evocation of a
world where things refuse to fit together, where terrible
things happen to the wrong people for the wrong reasons,
where horrors leap out of the most trivial or ridiculous con-
texts. The disjointedness of the narrative pattern reinforces

our sense of a nightmare world where everything is out of joint. Why should we expect aesthetic order when monkeys can chase people into their graves, green tea can cause damnation, and therapists can suddenly drop out of sight when patients are on the precipice of suicide? Besides instilling a sense of underlying chaos, the filtering device also gives the impression of narrative distance, a useful effect in any kind of ironic fiction, but particularly necessary in the ghost story, where too much narrative directness can instantly blunt the desired impact. Jennings must seem like a thoroughly helpless creature, dwarfed by diabolical forces beyond his comprehension (let alone control) and gradually receding from our vision into hell. What could serve this purpose better than to have his narrative manipulated by three verbose doctors who are more concerned with selling their theories than with protecting his sanity?

Le Fanu's complicated narrative skein also helps create the "loophole" of ambiguity mentioned by M. R. James. It is at least *possible* that Hesselius's claims are justified, that his unorthodox medications would have banished Jennings's monkey, and that his infallibility is "absolutely certain." (Although this certainty would not efface the supernatural element in the story, it would have the disappointing effect of a natural explanation: demonic forces might still exist in some sense, but would be so easily subdued by infallible German doctors as to be in effect naturalized.) For the many reasons mentioned, however, we doubt Hesselius's word: the easy way out is a remote possibility but "not quite practicable." Even if Hesselius were believable as the medical equivalent of a Dickensian benefactor (dispensing cures instead of money at the end), we would still be left with the terrible irony of Jennings destroying himself just as he is about to be delivered.

Either way, "Green Tea" is a horror tale. It is Le Fanu's most extreme, yet most controlled performance. Although the "well managed crescendo" admired by M. R. James occurs in most of his tales, nowhere is it more attenuated and cumulative than in "Green Tea." In "Schalken the Painter," "Chief Justice Harbottle" and others, the initial apparition comes fairly quickly; here the "journey" is more leisurely and spread out; the distance travelled is greater. By taking his time, Le-Fanu makes Jennings's "doors of perception" experience all the more painful and catastrophic. Similarly, the heavy use of ambiguity and dramatic irony suggests a dislocated, strangely modern world where reality is grim enough to outpace our most exaggerated fantasies. Though written in the late nineteenth century, "Green Tea," as E. F. Benson has happily put it, is "instinct with an awfulness which custom cannot stale."[16] Those who find ghost stories boring or silly will probably interpret "awfulness" in a different way than Benson intended. But the rest of us know exactly what he means.

CHAPTER II

BEGINNINGS: SHERIDAN LE FANU

In considering Le Fanu's work as a whole, further comparisons with Poe almost inevitably insinuate themselves. Poe's impact has been more scattered and diffuse than Le Fanu's: the fungi surrounding the House of Usher have grown into other fields, corroding everything from decadence poetry to existential philosophy. Le Fanu's influence extends only to other ghost story writers. Even here, his imprint is appropriately ghostly and indistinct. Part of the difficulty is that much of his work was published anonymously, but even the tales which were not are elusive; although his novels, poems, and journalism were reasonably well known in Ireland, most of his ghostly tales quickly dropped out of sight and remained that way for well over half a century. Even specialists in weird fiction were unaware of his work. Dorothy Scarborough's *The Supernatural in Modern Fiction* (1917), the pioneer study of the genre, contains not a word about Le Fanu, an omission analogous to leaving Emerson out of a comprehensive study of American Transcendentalism.[1] Lovecraft's *Supernatural Horror in Fiction* (1927) is almost as negligent, mentioning Le Fanu only once in a languidly confused passage which attempts to link him with Wells, Conan Doyle, and other representatives of "the romantic, semi-Gothic, quasi-moral tradition."[2] Part of this neglect was caused by the unavailability of texts: until E. F. Bleiler's recent Le Fanu edition appeared (1964), the author's tales were almost impossible to find, even in large university libraries. Bibliographical information was consequently either lacking or com-

32

pletely misleading, for bibliographers obviously did not know
what he had published. Even the *Cambridge History of
English Literature* (1917) lists only three works (*The House by
the Churchyard, Uncle Silas*, and *The Purcell Papers*) in its
bibliography of Le Fanu's fiction.[3]

One exception to this neglect is an early reference to Le
Fanu in an 1884 autobiographical volume by James Payn. The
reference occurs in the context of Payn's account of a visit
to the Duke of Albany:

> He was not a student in the ordinary sense of the word,
> though his knowledge of science and philosophy was probably much
> superior to mine, but he was well acquainted with the lighter bran-
> ches of literature and took great pleasure in them. I had the satis-
> faction of introducing him to the works of Le Fanu and his admiration
> of that author (so strangely neglected by the general public, notwith-
> standing the popularity of some of his imitators) vied with my own.[4]

The passage is particularly interesting in that Payn seems
aware not only of Le Fanu's works, but of his originality:
although stated parenthetically, the sneer at Le Fanu's "imi-
tators" appears to be the earliest recognition of his place in
the evolution of the genre.

Until the 1920's, this recognition was uncommon even
among ghostly writers. As far as documented evidence goes,
Henry James and M. R. James appear to be the first writers
to show an awareness of Le Fanu. In Henry James's "The
Liar," the narrator describes the bedroom of an English
country house in which "There was the customary novel of
Mr. Le Fanu for the bedside; the ideal reading in a country
house for the hours after midnight."[5] Even here the reference
is not to the horror tales, but to one of Le Fanu's fourteen
Gothic novels, elaborately plotted mysteries and romances
occasionally spiked with supernatural episodes.[6] Only M. R.
James, in his early introduction to Le Fanu (1923), seems to
have been aware of Le Fanu's role in shaping the modern
ghost story, a recognition which came fifty years after Le
Fanu's death.[7]

It is futile to argue whether Le Fanu was more influential
than Poe. The influence-hunting of modern criticism, always
a dubious game, is particularly irrelevant in a genre where

there is so little evidence that the writers read their "influential" predecessors. Several writers (Machen and de la Mare
are good examples) expressed an admiration for Poe, yet re-
jected his high-strung tone for the kind of understatement and
innuendo which was Le Fanu's distinct innovation. With the
exception of M. R. James and Bram Stoker (whose *Dracula*
was taken directly from Le Fanu's "Carmilla"), no one has acknowledged a direct Le Fanu influence. On the other hand,
those who have acknowledged a debt to M. R. James (notably
H. R. Wakefield and A. C. and E. F. Benson)[8] are indirectly
acknowledging a debt to Le Fanu, for James has always in-
sisted that he was merely working in the Le Fanu tradition.[9]
However it happened, whether through conscious imitation or
an independent rediscovery of the same aesthetic principle,
nearly all of the early twentieth-century writers in the field
paced and structured their narratives in the Le Fanu manner.

There is no Le Fanu biography, just as there is no extended
study of Le Fanu's horror tales. S. M. Ellis established most
of what is known of Le Fanu's life in his wonderfully entertaining book, *Wilkie Collins, Le Fanu and Others* (1931).
Other commentators, in recapitulating Ellis's research, have
also followed Ellis's example in interpreting the few known
facts to fit stereotypical notions of ghost story writers and
their lives. Nelson Browne, for example, has this to say about
Le Fanu's Irish boyhood:

> It is not difficult to discover in the circumstances of Le Fanu's boy-
> hood and youth the formative influences which made him the kind of
> writer he became. Everything he heard and saw was deeply rooted in
> a romantic past: the historic associations of Chapelizod and the mili-
> tary traditions of the Royal Hibernian school; the mysterious glen of
> Alberlow; the brooding grandeur of the Slieve Felim Mountains; the
> tales of banshees, changelings and pookhas; the traditional ballad
> singers; the literary inheritance that he had acquired from the Sher-
> idans; his father's urbane classical culture. All these things powerfully
> affected an imagination which was at one and the same time lively
> and reflective.[10]

Ellis's comment about Le Fanu's childhood "desire for se-
clusion" completes the picture: this kind of commentary, with
its emphasis on romantic surroundings and childhood loneli-
ness, is also a commonplace in accounts of later writers,

particularly Machen and Lovecraft.[11] As an attempt to explain why Le Fanu became a ghost story writer, the theory has a kind of vague applicability. At the same time, it is interesting how few traditional "banshees, changelings and pookhas" appear in Le Fanu's tales. E. F. Bleiler, in an astute introduction to the tales, makes the comment that "despite his Irish background, native Irish folklore seems to have meant little to him. . . . The few stories in which Le Fanu used true Irish Folklore are much his weakest work."[12] The bulk of Le Fanu's mature works such as "Carmilla" and "Green Tea" have little to do with Irish sources.

Bleiler's point, it should be added, has wide applicability. Yeats's Michael Robartes tales, for example, are more ghostly than anything in *The Celtic Twilight*. Writers like Blackwood, Machen, and Asquith, when they used folklore, used only fragments which they imported from anywhere and often mixed or distorted, creating a collage effect not unlike the works of Eliot, Ives, Bartok and other artists of the period. Even the more traditional writers did their best to transcend the tradition they ostensibly worked within, often resorting to the inversion of a hackneyed theme. Monsignor R. H. Benson (private chamberlain to Pope Pius X) once wrote a haunted-house story about a house haunted by nothingness: "I don't think that I felt there was any presence there or anything of that kind. It was rather the opposite; it was the feeling of an extraordinary emptiness. . . . Like a Catholic cathedral in Protestant hands. . . ." Furthermore, many of the most frequently anthologized tales, such as F. Marion Crawford's "The Upper Berth" or L. P. Hartley's "The Travelling Grave," are entirely free from folklore underpinnings.

As in the case of many writers, Le Fanu's life does not explain his works. The reverse process has more validity: the terrible sense of moroseness and isolation in late tales such as "Green Tea" and "The Familiar" may serve as an emotional clue to the darkness of Le Fanu's later years, years so frequently alluded to by Ellis, Browne, and others who have tried to fashion an archetypal image for his life and art. The need to do so seems all the more compelling in view of the apparent uneventfulness of Le Fanu's early years. Despite the richness of his surroundings, Le Fanu, like Machen and M. R. James, appears to have led a disappointingly undramatic early life. His family history is a record of banal successes, punctuated only by several attacks during the Tithe War. Born in 1814 to a middle-class Dublin family of Huguenot descent, he graduated from Trinity College, studied law for a brief time, successfully edited several newspapers and periodicals (notably the *Dublin University Magazine*), and married happily in 1844. He published his first ghost story at the age of twenty-three ("The Ghost and the Bone Setter") and followed it up with several more, although he published only one collection of his tales during this period. [13]

After the premature death of his wife in 1858, Le Fanu's life changed dramatically. Irrevocably depressed by the loss, he became a total recluse, living a strange life which furnished the material for Ellis's memorable account of his last years. According to Ellis, who used Le Fanu's son Brinsley as a valuable source, Le Fanu became increasingly obsessed with the supernatural. His mystery novels, notably *The House By the Churchyard* (1863) and *Uncle Silas* (1864), became noticeably more pessimistic and more generously laced with ghostly episodes. In "The Haunting of the Tiled House" in *The House By the Churchyard*, the inhabitants of the house are invaded by an evil force manifested by a plump white hand resembling a malignant toad. Le Fanu's most enduring achievements during this period were his horror tales, which he produced with far greater frequency after his wife's death.

The most quotable passage in Ellis's book deals with Brinsley's account of how his father wrote these late chillers. It is an extraordinary tale:

> He wrote mostly in his bed at night, using copy-books for his manuscript. He always had two candles by his side on a small table; one of these dimly glimming tapers would be left burning while he took a brief sleep. Then, when he awoke about 2 a.m. amid the darkling shadows of the heavy furnishings and hangings of his old-fashioned room, he would brew himself some strong tea—which he drank copiously and frequently throughout the day—and write for a couple of hours in that eerie period of the night when human vitality is at its lowest ebb and the Powers of Darkness rampant and terrifying. What wonder then, that, with his brain ever peopled by day and by night with mysterious and terrible beings, he became afflicted by

horrible dreams, which, as I have suggested, were the bases of his last stories of the supernatural.[14]

Le Fanu's method involved a kind of mad circularity. His nightmares inspired tales which in turn inspired more nightmares. According to Ellis's anecdote, they also inspired his death and in doing so transformed the author into the role of the classic victim in one of his own tales. Like Roderick Usher, Le Fanu cultivated his own accelerating paranoia. He had frequent nightmares during his last years, and was particularly troubled by a repetitive dream of a large Victorian house collapsing on him in his sleep. He died (of a heart attack) very much like Barton in "The Familiar"—in his bed with his eyes bugging out in an expression of horrendous panic. "I feared this," said Le Fanu's doctor, "That house fell at last."[15] No other ghost story writer has been blessed with such an appropriate death.[16]

Unfortunately, Le Fanu's development as a writer is not as dramatic as his death would suggest. It lacks a sense of cumulative progression. An erratic writer, Le Fanu leaped ahead as frequently as he doubled back on himself: the distribution of continuities and contrasts between the early and late tales is haphazard, precluding easy generalizations about early, middle, or late "periods" in his career. He was as capable of writing the masterful "Schalken the Painter" in 1839 as he was of writing the awkward, unconvincing "Dickon the Devil" in 1872. Nevertheless, the Hesselius tales (all of which are collected in *In a Glass Darkly*) have a sense of assurance, control, and maniacal intensity which are absent in most of the earlier work.[17] The Hesselius tales also segregate themselves from the other tales by their denser narrative texture and the more clinical tracing of supernatural "stages." Even so, they cannot be said to represent a definitive "late manner," for none of the other late tales exhibit these characteristics.[18] What they do represent is a noticeable thickening and development of motifs from the earlier work.

A sense of grim absurdity, for example, is apparent in the earliest tales. In "Schalken the Painter," (1839), the innocent sixteen-year-old Rose Velderkaust is remorselessly and inexplicably victimized, much as Jennings is. Her forced marriage to the corpselike (but wealthy) Minheer Vanderhausen seems profoundly uncalled-for and undeserved. Rose never escapes from this otherworldly rapist either in this life or, as Schalken's dream vision implies, in the next. The "arch smile" she displays as she draws the black curtains on the four-poster coffin—revealing "the livid and demoniac form of Vanderhausen"—suggests she has eternally succumbed to his advances. She hardly has any choice in the matter.

This sense of helplessness in a malign universe, the major theme of *In A Glass Darkly*, appears throughout the earlier tales, although sometimes obliquely. An example is "Ghost Stories of the Tiled House," which is told in the deceptively pleasant context of one of Old Sally's fireside yarns.[19] In this tale, a two-year-old child is driven to insanity (diagnosed as "incipient water on the brain") by an invading white hand which is enigmatically connected with a distant relative's childhood trauma. The earlier experience occurred in "a haunted nursery" where the relative was terrorized by a "fat and pale" apparition in laced clothes, presumably the owner of the hand (407). The nature of the connection is never revealed, nor is the identity of the apparition.[20]

This quality of threatening inscrutability injects even the non-apparitional early tales with a dark stream of supernatural horror. Though there is nothing overtly supernatural in "The Last Heir of Castle Connor" (1838), the suicidal death of the young hero at the hands of a mysterious professional dueller has a mesmeric, choreographed quality suggestive of a diabolical ritual. [21] It is only when he is at "the very verge of the fathomless pit of death" that the victim suddenly becomes keenly alert, as if awakening from a nightmare into something far worse:

> Never before or since have I seen horror so intensely depicted. It seemed actually as if O'Conner's mind had been unsettled by a shock: the few words he uttered were marked with all the incoherence of distraction; but it was not words that marked his despair most strongly; the appalling and heart-sickening groans, I might almost say *howls*, that came from the terror-stricken and dying man must haunt me while I live; the expression, too, of hopeless imploring agony with which he turned his eyes from object to object, I can never forget.[22]

This is easily one of the most dreadful death scenes in Le Fanu, equalling if not transcending the final agony of James Barton in "The Familiar." The vision of death as a "fathomless pit" is communicated with far greater authenticity and conviction than the reconciliatory message delivered by O'Connor's mother at the end of the tale: "I doated upon him—I idolized him—I thought too little of other holier affections; and God may have taken him from me, only to teach me, by this severe lesson, that I owed to heaven a larger share of my heart than to anything earthly."[23] Le Fanu appears to be faking it here. On the other hand, it is possible that he meant this speech to serve as an ironic commentary on the hollowness of the narrator's Christian "resignation." In any case, the tension between the artificially injected faith in Christian redemption and the more dramatically realized terror of the void reflects a painfully divided consciousness.

This splintered consciousness segregates plot from theme, imagery from soliloquy, in much of the earlier work. In a tale like "The Fortunes of Sir Robert Ardagh," the resultant counterpoint complicates the texture and heightens the reader's interest. When a contradiction exists between a writer's conscious message and subconscious feelings, the prose often takes on a new dimension, as Lawrence has shown in his reading of *The Scarlet Letter*. Occasionally, however, the strain becomes too great and threatens to tear the fabric of the story apart. "The Mysterious Lodger" is a case in point.

This is perhaps the most obscure of Le Fanu's ghost stories. M. R. James refused to reprint it in *Madam Crowl's Ghost and Other Tales of Mystery* on the grounds that the tale is more of a religious allegory than a ghost story. Implicit in his refusal is the assumption that the two are incompatible, and indeed they are. To the extent that Le Fanu relies on allegory, his characteristic ghostliness is undermined. The story tells of the conversion of the freethinking narrator from the influence of "Voltaire, Tom Paine, Hume, Shelley, and the whole school of infidels, poetical as well as prose,"[24] to the "sweet and hallowed influence" of Christianity."[25] The conversion is inversely accomplished through the invasion of a demon masquerading as a new lodger; this "abhorred being" terrorizes the household, mouths endless blasphemies, sows "evil thoughts" concerning the validity of Biblical teaching, tricks the narrator into committing the "unforgivable sin" against the Holy Ghost, and finally murders the narrator's two children by breathing into their faces. He is finally opposed by another mysterious stranger, this one bearing a Christ-like rather than a demonic countenance. The narrator understandably converts to Christianity.

All this is a bit much, especially for Le Fanu, who rarely clutters his stories with allegorical machinery. In *In A Glass Darkly*, allegory disappears almost entirely. As Le Fanu's only sustained allegory, "The Mysterious Lodger" is revealing in that it does not work even on its own terms. Since the narrator recovers his faith well before the death of his second child, the second death seems horribly gratuitous in light of the Christ figure's final intimation that he had the power to banish the demon any time he pleased. Indeed the demon's sneering commentary seems entirely appropriate: "You have buried your little daughter this morning. It requires a good deal of that new attribute of yours, *faith*, which judges all things by a rule of contraries, and can never see anything but kindness in the worst afflictions which malignity could devise, to discover benignity and mercy in the torturing calamity which has just punished you and your wife for *nothing!*"[26] On some level, Le Fanu must concur with this speech. He continually manipulates the plot in ways which not only undercut the logic of the allegory, but which seem to support the most heretical proclamations of the demon. The child is not only buried for nothing but, in a perversely Poe-like twist, is accidentally buried alive. It is as if Le Fanu wants to affirm the Christ figure, but finds the demon more compelling and authentic. What begins as a religious allegory becomes a grotesque parody of one. Even the anticipated banishment scene never materializes; the narrator simply flees from the house, leaving the demon with the option of tormenting future occupants, which he duly seizes. As usual in Le Fanu, evil prevails. The house, in effect, becomes haunted, and there doesn't seem to be much the angelic stranger can do about it. A bizarre analogy is drawn at the end between the vulnerability of old houses and the position of women in a sexist society: ". . . the reputation of a house, like that of a woman, once blown upon never quite recovers."[27]

It should be added that the reader, to the extent that he ignores the allegory (which Le Fanu in effect does himself), should not find this tale to be as problematic as James does. Le Fanu's lodger, with his "sinister, black scratch-wig," his "odious green goggles" (a strange premonition of the disguise of Wells's Invisible Man), and his shadowy co-conspirator, is a fascinating creation. Le Fanu thought well enough of him to repeat several of his more atrocious mannerisms—such as his habit of blasphemously interrupting the narrator's prayer—in the monkey's behavior in "Green Tea."

There are other early horrors on which Le Fanu plays variations in the later tales. His favorite device in evoking these creatures is the use of obsessively repeating image clusters which conjoin malignance, sensuality, glowing redness, and leering insanity, either all at once or in endless permutations and combinations: the spectre in "The Sexton's Adventure" (1851) is surrounded by "a wonderful red glow, which duskily illuminated his entire figure like a lurid atmosphere of meteor";[28] the sinister valet in "The Fortunes of Sir Robert Ardagh" (1838) is described in terms of his "fearful scowl" which is "half demonic, half insane" (351); Judge Harbottle appears in "Strange Disturbances In Aungier Street" bearing a "stony face with its infernal lineaments of malignity and despair, gloating" on the narrator with a "sensual" and "unspeakably dreadful" (375-76) smile; the apparition who absconds with the lovely Una (another heroine abducted by a dead man) in "Ultor de Lacy" boasts "a very long sickly face with a drooping nose, and a sly sarcastic leer, and a great purplish stain over-spreading more than half of one cheek" (451).

The tendency in the Hesselius tales is to unravel these characteristics gradually, in carefully structured "stages," rather than deliver them in undifferentiated bursts of adjectives and metaphors. On the other hand, the early tales have a kind of fluid, improvisatory quality that the more carefully nuanced

Hesselius tales lack. Furthermore, it is possible to turn up passages in Le Fanu's earliest efforts which are as deftly controlled as similar passages in "Carmilla" or "Green Tea."

It is hard to imagine, for example, anything in Le Fanu more threatening than the description of the suitor who suddenly appears to pursue the hand of Rose in "Schalken the Painter":

> A quantity of grizzled hair descended in long tresses from his head, and rested upon the plaits of a stiff ruff, which effectually concealed his neck. So far all was well; but the face!—all the flesh was coloured with the bluish leaden hue, which is sometimes produced by metallic medicines, administered in excessive quantities; the eyes showed an undue proportion of muddy white, and had a certain indefinable character of insanity; the hue of the lips bearing the usual relation to that of the face, was sensual, malignant, and even satanic. It was remarkable that the worshipful stranger suffered as little as possible of his flesh to appear, and that during his visit he did not once remove his gloves. . . . There was something indescribably odd, even horrible, about all his motions, something undefinable, that was unnatural, unhuman; it was as if the limbs were guided and directed by a spirit unused to the management of bodily machinery. The stranger spoke hardly at all during his visit, which did not exceed half an hour; and the host himself could scarcely muster courage enough to utter the few necessary salutations and courtesies; and, indeed, such was the nervous terror which the presence of Vanderhausen inspired, that very little would have made all his entertainers fly in downright panic from the room. They had not so far lost self-possession, however, as to fail to observe two strange peculiarities of their visitor. During his stay his eyelids did not once close, or, indeed, move in the slightest degree; and farther, there was a deathlike stillness in his whole person, owing to the absence of the heaving motion of the chest, caused by the process of respiration. These two peculiarities, though when told they may appear trifling, produced a very striking and unpleasant effect when seen and observed. (38-39)

The combination of intentional vagueness (the "certain indefinable character of insanity" in the eyes) and clinical explicitness (the "bluish leaden hue which is sometimes produced by metallic medicines" in the face), concealing the very thing it seeks to clarify, is characteristic of Le Fanu's later style. We get just enough information to conjure up the spectre in our imaginations, but no more. The failure of the stranger to even "once remove his gloves"—a definitive Le Fanu touch—looks forward not just to the later tales, but to the sardonic attenuations of L. P. Hartley, Elizabeth Bowen, and Ramsey

Campbell. Also apparent in the passage is a kind of mad, though oddly understated, humor. After noting that the stranger never blinks or breathes, the narrator adds apologetically that these characteristics "may appear trifling." This kind of ironic aside always signals Le Fanu's recognition that the most hideous apparitions are also, ineluctably, the funniest. Bursts of absurd humor occur throughout the early tales. Often, as in "Schalken," the humor occurs in basic plot situations, reinforcing our sense of the victim's hopelessness. When Rose finally manages to escape from the loathsome embrace of Vanderhausen, she issues "repeated injunctions" to her guardian and her minister not to leave her alone, after which they almost immediately proceed to leave her alone. The ever-watchful demon wastes no time of course in sweeping her out the window, just as the monkey wastes no time closing in on Jennings after he is deserted by Hesselius. A strong element of farce obtains in both cases, saturating the plots with an added element of doom and horror. Le Fanu's tales suggest a world in which we are unbearably alone in situations of escalating awfulness: our friends desert us, not when they would be useful, but when they are indispensable.

Le Fanu makes us feel this sense of aloneness through the use of constant ironies. In "The Familiar," James Barton, a former agnostic, seeks the help of a "famous clergyman"; he is told by this august spiritual advocate that the demon pursuing him is merely an hallucination caused by "the undue action or torpidity of one or other" of Barton's "bodily organs." (225). This is a typical Le Fanu reversal. When the atheists in these stories are awakened by demons in their beds, they undergo rapid conversions; but the spiritual advisors whose help they seek and whose theology they embrace suddenly assume the role of hard-line materialists, rebuffing them with Hobbesian severity.

It is significant that Le Fanu's first published ghost story, "The Ghost and the Bone Setter" (1838), is his most intensely farcical. This delightful story tells of the havoc unleashed by the ghost of an old squire who bootlegs cold water to "allay the burning thirst of purgatory."[30] To obtain the much-sought-after liquid, he periodically comes down out of his picture. He is considerably more mobile than other picture ghosts: the ghost in M. R. James's "The Mezzotint" merely skulks from one end of the picture to the other, while Hawthorne's "Edward Randolph's Portrait" can do no more than stare down from the wall with a progressively sour expression. The squire is not content to go after water; he also raids the liquor cabinet, pitching a noisy, bottle-smashing drunk before staggering back to his frame.

The brief introduction, which explains the Irish superstition behind the story, is almost as comical as the story itself. According to the superstition, "the corpse last buried" in a given churchyard, is "obliged" to supply "his brother tenants with fresh water." This belief has resulted over the years in much grim hilarity:

> Fierce and desperate conflicts have ensued in the case of two funeral parties approaching the same churchyard together, each endeavoring to secure to his own dead priority of sepulture and in consequence immunity from the tax levied upon the pedestrian powers of the last comer. An instance not long since occurred, in which one of two such parties, through fear of losing to their deceased friend this inestimable advantage, made their way to the churchyard by a *short cut*, and in violation of one of their strongest prejudices, actually threw the coffin over the wall, lest time should be lost in making their entrance through the gate.[31]

The objection may be raised that this is merely a whimsical story, in an entirely different category from the later, more serious tales. But the difference, is one of degree and context only. Had the squire been a malignant rather than a harmless ghost, he would be not unlike the drunken phantom in "The Sexton's Adventure," a tale as dark and horrific as any, but also studded with grotesque humor.

The climax of this tendency is *In A Glass Darkly,* tales which are consistently ironic, which open vistas of cosmic horror from trivial or laughable premises. "Mr. Justice Harbottle," "The Familiar," and "Carmilla" are trickier than "Green Tea" in that the moral elements give the illusion of moving toward a manageable allegorical resolution. In "Mr. Justice Harbottle" the illusion is short-lived. It is the most violent of Le Fanu's tales, with a torture scene clinical enough to arouse the most sadistic reader. But it also conjures up a deeper, more comprehensive cruelty which undermines its didactic surface.

"Mr. Justice Harbottle" was one of Le Fanu's final convulsing visions. Yet this was not the first time Le Fanu had used Justice Harbottle as a character. In a much earlier tale, "An Account of Some Strange Disturbances in Aungier Street" (1853), the deceased Judge appears on a staircase as a monstrous bloated rat. Although Le Fanu did not get around to killing him off until twenty years later, he must have been pleased with the fiendish death he finally conceived for him in "Mr. Justice Harbottle." It is characteristic of Le Fanu's eccentricity that he gave us the apparition before the live character. On the other hand, there is nothing unusual about his use of the same concept in different tales: if the idea is ghostly enough, he is reluctant to drop it after one development.[32]

At first glance, the plot has a more comforting logic than the plot of "Green Tea." The central character, Harbottle, is a law-and-order hanging judge, "as dangerous and unscrupulous" as he is corrupt, a sadist who delights in sending innocent men to the hangman (248). Going a step further than Dickens in *Bleak House,* Le Fanu presents Harbottle as a typical administrator of the English criminal code, which he envisions as "a rather pharisaical, bloody, and heinous system of justice" (254). One evening, the judge is visited by a mysterious man of "unnaturally chalky" appearance who warns him of a "wicked conspiracy" against his life (251). The next premonition occurs in court when the judge sees an emaciated figure with "a stripe of swollen blue round his neck" grinning at him with a "faint thin-lipped smile" from the side of the courtroom· while grimly twisting his head from side to side (259). The apparition, who uncomfortably resembles Lewis Pyneweck, a man Harbottle has sent to the gallows, hands a letter to the court crier, then mysteriously disappears. The letter is an extraordinary indictment issued by an "Officer of the Crown Solicitor in the Kingdom of Life and Death," demanding Harbottle's appearance at the "High Court of Appeal" to be tried for "the murder of one Lewis Pyneweck of

Shrewsbury," "wrongfully executed" on a bogus forgery charge
(260). (Harbottle, engaged in an affair with Pyneweck's wife,
had apparently sent Pyneweck to the gallows out of sheer
meanness.) The indictment explicitly sets the trial for the
tenth day of the month. Late on the evening of the ninth,
while driving in his carriage, Harbottle is abducted by two
"evil-looking fellows, each with a pistol in his hand, and
dressed like Bow Street officers" (263). In "utter amaze-
ment," Harbottle recognizes one of them as "Dingly Chuff,
fifteen years ago a footman in his service, whom he had
turned off at a moment's notice, in a burst of jealousy, and
indicted for a missing spoon. The man had died in prison of
the jail-fever" (263). Harbottle is driven to a decaying court-
house where he is arraigned and tried for murder. Except
for their glowing eyes, the ghostly jurors are invisible in the
dark courtroom but are probably of the same avenging company as Chuff and Pyneweck. Predictably, they find the
prisoner guilty, and the stern judge, Chief-Justice Twofold,
arranges the tenth of the next month as the execution date.
Before releasing him, the officers of the court torture the
prisoner with red-hot irons. Bellowing with pain, Harbottle
awakens himself from what was apparently a nightmare. The
following month, his doctor finds him "sinking into the state
of nervous dejection in which men lose their faith in orthodox
advice, and in despair consult quacks, astrologers, and nursery
story-tellers" (268). The doctor is convinced that his patient
is only "troubled with hypochondria," but Mrs. Pyneweck, her
daughter, and the scullery maid think differently on the
evening of the ninth when each of them independently runs
into one of the ghostly avengers from Harbottle's dream.
According to their witness, the house is being invaded by
strange pallid men in black who carry chains and hanging
ropes. Not surprisingly, Judge Harbottle is found dead the
next morning, hanging by his neck from a banister. Citing
"medical evidence," of his "atrabilious state," an autopsy
establishes suicide as the cause of death (273).

The plot gives us a beautifully worked out scheme of poetic
justice in which the punishment exactly fits the crime.
Le Fanu even makes Chief Justice Twofold a double of

Harbottle, thus injecting the traditional death symbolism of
doubles with a nice ironic sting. Since Harbottle (unlike
Jennings) is a thorough-going villain who gets what he deserves, the world of the story is ostensibly different from the
world of "Green Tea."

However, if we read the central dream sequence carefully, we begin to suspect that the difference is superficial.
Even though the wicked judge is finally brought to justice
by those whom he has wronged, there is still something profoundly out of joint in this visionary trial scene:

> If this was the High Court of Appeal, which never rose day or night,
> it might account for the pale and jaded aspect of everybody in it. An
> air of indescribable gloom hung upon the pallid features of all the
> people here; no one ever smiled; all looked more or less secretly
> suffering. . . .
> Where upon the chief-justice laughed suddenly, and every one in
> court, turning round upon the prisoner, laughed also, till the laugh
> grew and roared all round like a deafening acclamation; he saw
> nothing but glittering eyes and teeth, a universal stare and grin; but
> though all the voices laughed, not a single face of all those that con-
> centrated their gaze upon him looked like a laughing face. The mirth
> subsided as suddenly as it began. . . .
> Nothing the prisoner could argue, cite, or state, was permitted to
> retard for a moment the march of the case towards its catastrophe.
> The chief-justice seemed to feel his power over the jury, and to
> exult and riot in the display of it. He glared at them, he nodded to
> them; he seemed to have established an understanding with them.
> The lights were faint in that part of the court. The jurors were mere
> shadows, sitting in rows; the prisoner could see a dozen pair of white
> eyes shining, coldly, out of the darkness; and whenever the judge in
> his charge, which was contemptuously brief, nodded and grinned and
> gibed, the prisoner could see, in the obscurity, by the dip of all these
> rows of eyes together, that the jury nodded in acquiescence.
> And now the charge was over, the huge chief-justice leaned back
> panting and gloating on the prisoner. Every one in the court turned
> about, and gazed with steadfast hatred on the man in the dock. From
> the jury-box where the twelve sworn brethren were whispering to-
> gether, a sound in the general stillness like a prolonged "hiss-s-s!"
> was heard; and then, in answer to the challenge of the officer, "How
> say you, gentlemen of the jury, guilty or not guilty?" came in a
> melancholy voice the finding, "Guilty."
> The place seemed to the eyes of the prisoner to grow gradually
> darker and darker, till he could discern nothing distinctly but the
> lumen of the eyes that were turned upon him from every bench and
> side and corner and gallery of the building.

The judge and jurors in the High Court of Appeal are

clearly not ministers of divine justice. It makes no sense to
view them as we would the ghost in *Hamlet*, as tragically
wronged spirits seeking their just revenge. The imagery in this
fantastic dream is exactly parallel to the imagery which we
associate with Jennings's monkeyish tormenter: the same eyes
glowing from an obscure bleakness, the same peculiar aura
of langour and stupefaction, the same twisted grins and mirthless laughs. These diabolical associations are manifested
whenever these figures appear, no matter who sees them.
But this imagery is inconsistent with the innocence of the
accusers, an innocence which is essential to the judge's
villainy and thus to any moral interpretation of the tale. If
Chuff, Pyneweck, and the other spectral jurors are innocent,
why are they suffering the torments of the guilty? Why are
they brought to life with the language Le Fanu reserves for
demons? It is awful enough for Chuff to rot his life away in
jail for stealing a spoon, but obscene that he should then be
damned for it. Wretched as he is, Hamlet's father is at worst
in Limbo or Purgatory, but these creatures are clearly part of
Le Fanu's "enormous machinery of hell." They pass their
sentence not with a sense of moral outrage or solemn justice,
but with sadistic glee, after which they torture their victim in
a singularly revolting fashion. Like the monkey in "Green
Tea" (with whom they seem to have a loathsome kinship),
they are the agents of an "atrocious plan" which has implications we are never allowed to grasp.

From no point of view do the jagged pieces in this
puzzle fit together to form a Victorian fictional pattern
of cause and effect. If the judge's accusers are innocent
victims, they should not personify damnation; if they are
guilty, the judge should not be a villain; if they were all
sent to hell independently for other crimes entirely, the story
collapses completely, for we are given no evidence of such
crimes. The tale is all the more slippery in that the plot ingre-
dients which suggest a metaphor for Old Testament revenge
morality—the judge's corruption and wealth, the avengers'
innocence and poverty—almost mix well. Le Fanu uses these
appearances of order the same way he uses forbidden books
and strong tea: as a way of teasing us into thinking that his

horrors have a tidy, explainable reason behind their eruption. That he never allows us to think this way for long says something about the uncanny effectiveness of these tales. No matter how skillfully it is accomplished, the transformation from the natural to the supernatural world is not what really disturbs us. (There have been too many ghosts in literature for us to be shaken by their mere appearance.) More chilling is the transformation from supernatural order to supernatural horror.

The modern ghost story conjures up an inexplicably horrible world whose inhabitants follow their own mysterious rules. The only principle of consistency seems to be a self-referential system of cruelty, capable of constantly regenerating itself as it seeps into the natural order of things. Occasionally, as in "Mr. Justice Harbottle," a story will show it operating with equal intensity in both worlds, in which case the supernatural disturbance echoes what is already apparent in everyday reality. Even in this case there is not necessarily a rational, causal relation between abominations in this world and the next: Harbottle, an inhabitant of the normal, empirical world, incarcerates and kills people, largely because he enjoys it; he is then apprehended by similarly fiendish figures from another world who revile, torture, and kill him also because they enjoy it. The two events are joined together by mechanical elements in the plot, but the memorable thing is the gleeful cruelty inherent in each event. The symbolic center of this world is brilliantly visualized in the "gigantic gallows" which tower in the darkness of Harbottle's dream: replete with an endless supply of dangling corpses and an eager hangman who shakes a rope and cries out at Harbottle with "a voice high and distant as the caw of a raven hovering over a gibbet," this eternal death machine is a perfect metaphor for Le Fanu's vision of reality (264).

Structurally, "Mr. Justice Harbottle" bears many similarities to "Green Tea." Although Hesselius does not appear as a character, his diagnosis of the case appears in the prologue:

"It was one of the best declared cases of an opening of the interior sense, which I have met with. It was affected too, by the phenomenon, which occurs so frequently as to indicate a law of these eccentric conditions; that is to say, it exhibited what I may term, the contagious character of this sort of intrusion of the spirit-world upon the proper domain of matter. So soon as the spirit-action has established itself in the case of one patient, its developed energy begins to radiate, more or less effectually, upon the others. The interior vision of the child was opened; as was, also, that of its mother, Mrs. Pyneweck; and both the interior vision and hearing of the scullery-maid, were opened on the same occasion. After-appearances are the result of the law explained in Vol. II, Section 17 to 49. The common centre of association, simultaneously recalled, unites, or *re*unites, as the case may be, for a period measured, as we see, in Section 37. The *maximum* will extend to days, the *minimum* is little more than a second. We see the operation of this principle perfectly displayed, in certain cases of lunacy, of epilepsy, and of mania, of a peculiar and painful character, though unattended by incapacity of business." (244-45)

We have already seen this kind of diagnosis in "Green Tea." As an awkward but fascinating attempt to fuse the ghostly with the scientific, the rational with the mystical, it anticipates several of the more bizarre "findings" of the Society for Psychical Research.[33] Although Hesselius's tone is characteristically dogmatic and pedantic, his absolutism (based on the "laws" he cites from his own book) is particularly strained here in that he never knew Harbottle or any of the other characters in the story. The diagnosis is based entirely on second-hand information; nevertheless, it serves Hesselius's function of imposing a desperate (ultimately unconvincing) order on the chaos which the story unleashes. Any one who has read many ghost stories knows what a common device this becomes by the early twentieth century: Blackwood and Machen are especially fond of dragging in oracular doctors who make quasi-scientific pronouncements on mysterious occurrences.

The prologue thus confirms what it wants to deny—that the Harbottle horrors are unexplainable. In its failure to codify and explain, the prologue reveals the irrelevance of anticipated arguments for and against "natural" or "supernatural" interpretations of the story. The difference between psychological ghosts and real ghosts is eliminated because the story forces us to glimpse a world in which such nice distinctions do not have any relevance. Skulking through that world—and breaking through into ours—are unearthly energies which are

neither material nor spiritual, but a hideous synthesis resis-
tant to classification and analysis. By trying to separate the
"spirit world" from the "proper domain of nature," Hesselius actually shows that the two lose their individuality once
the "intrusion" takes place. The perception of otherworldly
beings by several characters can no more be used to support
a "supernatural" interpretation of this tale than Jennings's
perception of the monkey can be used to support a "psychological" version of "Green Tea." In both stories, the line sep-
arating such categories is smudged. Beginning with Le Fanu,
one of the distinctive features of modern ghostly fiction is
precisely this synthesis of psychology and supernaturalism.
The dissolving of distinctions is connected with the overall
rupture of causality, the failure of the story to reveal any
underlying rationale behind the supernatural mechanism even
though the mechanism itself is minutely described. And
despite Hesselius's allusions to his own self-proclaimed laws,
we never know why some characters experience "an opening
of the interior sense" while others are mercifully spared this
second sight. We are given just enough information to con-
vince us that the experience is authentic, but never quite
enough to exorcise the experience through reason. Speci-
ficity has an ominous way of leading to vagueness, always
with the implication that the reader is finally as ignorant of
diabolical truth as the victim in the story and therefore as
vulnerable. In the prologue, for example, we are given specific details about the hauntingly "contagious character of this
sort of intrusion," but we never know why Jennings is not
similarly contagious even though "the phenomenon . . .
occurs so frequently as to indicate a law of these eccentric
conditions"(244).

Le Fanu's use of these visionary chain reactions is worth
special mention in that it demonstrates his innovativeness in
working out the kind of supernatural psychology so frequently attributed to other writers.[34] The most significant
assertion it calls into question is Leon Edel's point about
Henry James's original contribution to the genre:

> This was James's great discovery—that certain people who see ghosts
> —or witches, goblins, elves—become as it were contagious. They are

not only haunted—they haunt. In this way James added a new dimension to the tale of terror: he showed the contagion of fear.[35]

Le Fanu had already documented "the contagious character"
of uncanny experiences—almost anticipating Edel's very
words. Indeed, if we pursue the matter, we find Le Fanu
using the "contagion of fear" theme in several pre-Hesselius
tales—notably "Schalken the Painter" and "Ultor de Lacy."

Le Fanu's insistence on narrative distance—another trait he
shares with James—is sometimes excessive in the late tales.
Even more than "Green Tea," "Mr. Justice Harbottle" is
a jumble of editorial insertions, paraphrased letters, and
introductions to introductions. The familiar heavy hand of an
unknown editor (presumably the Hesselius "enthusiast" who
edited "Green Tea") is much in evidence: his narrative introduces another narrative which in turn introduces a letter
from an unnamed friend of the second narrator; the letter
introduces memories of childhood tales "heard recounted at
the fireside at home, with so delightful a horror" (248).

Although there is perhaps some attempt in all this to
achieve a mythical or at least folkloric perspective, the
attempt is undercut by the clinical separation of each thread
in the narrative fabric, as well as by the patently artificial
medical jargon crammed in by the editor to cover for the loss
of a more accurate "scientific" version. If the purpose of
myth is to interpret and clarify fundamental experiences, these
tales can almost be seen as antimythical: they move toward
shadowy uncertainty rather than clarification. There is
something almost Conradian in the seemingly senseless confusion of tales within tales, in the endless circling around an
experience which becomes progressively murky. Like Conrad
twenty years later, Le Fanu sees life as having an opacity,
a heart of darkness. As the metaphor for a world view,
Le Fanu's supernaturalism is not as far from Conrad's skepticism as we might think; they are simply different ways of
pinpointing vertigo and disorder.

Besides the narrative convolutions, there are other kinks
in the shape of Le Fanu's tales. The structure of ghostly
fiction has frequently been misunderstood as a predictable

linear movement from everyday reality to supernatural reality, the accretion of strange events always thickening into a crescendo, the climax always exploding at the end.[36] It is true that the openings are usually leisurely, the supernatural intrusion usually gradual; but it is also true that there is often more than one crescendo and that the climax does not always occur at the end. Though the fiendish intruder usually crawls slowly and ominously from the shadows of the story, he occasionally parades unabashedly into the daylight of the opening pages, slinking away again before any climax has had a chance to build. Le Fanu gives us a basic pattern, then twists and distorts it in different stories so that the reader is surprised in a variety of unpleasant ways even though he knows basically what is going to happen.

"Mr. Justice Harbottle" has several such surprises. Once the story gets underway, Le Fanu gives us an apparition scene almost immediately rather than building to it. (The vampire in "Carmilla" also makes an early appearance in the opening pages.) Introducing the anonymous character who has the vision as "a dry, sad, quiet man, who had known better days, and had always maintained an unexceptional character" (a typical Le Fanu seer), the narrator wastes no words telling us what the man saw:

> Unable to sleep, he had lighted a candle, and after having read for a time, had laid the book beside him. He heard the old clock at the stairhead strike one; and very shortly after, to his alarm he saw the closet-door, which he thought he had locked, open stealthily, and a slight dark man, particularly sinister, and somewhere about fifty, dressed in mourning of a very antique fashion, such a suit as we see in Hogarth, entered the room on tip-toe. He was followed by an elder man, stout, and blotched with scurvy, and whose features, fixed as a corpse's, were stamped with dreadful force with a character of sensuality and villainy.
>
> This old man wore a flowered silk dressing-gown and ruffles, and he remarked a gold ring on his finger, and on his head a cap of velvet, such as, in the days of perukes, gentlemen wore in undress.
>
> This direful old man carried in his ringed and ruffled hand a coil of rope; and these two figures crossed the floor diagonally, passing the foot of his bed, from the closet door at the farther end of the room, at the left, near the window, to the door opening upon the lobby, close to the bed's head, at his right.
>
> He did not attempt to describe his sensations as these figures

passed so near him. He merely said that so far from sleeping in that room again, no consideration the world could offer would induce him so much as to enter it again alone, even in the daylight. . . .

In answer to a question of mine, he said that neither appeared the least conscious of his presence. They did not seem to glide, but walked as living men do, but without any sound, and he felt a vibration on the floor as they crossed it. He so obviously suffered from speaking about the apparitions, that I asked him no more questions. (246-47)

The striking thing about this passage is that Le Fanu manages to make these figures both ghostly and physical. They do not glide or float about like old-fashioned ghosts, but walk "as living men do," causing physical vibrations without making actual sounds (a wonderfully bizarre distinction).

But this scene is only an atmospheric prelude to the main action. After the opening jolt, Le Fanu quickly relaxes the tension by introducing the letter which purports to explain the background of the apparition. The letter establishes the beginning of another crescendo, this time gradually building it toward Harbottle's terrifying dream. When Harbottle awakens, the intensity collapses, then rapidly builds to the visions of the servants and shuts off again at the abrupt, darkly predictable conclusion. Besides having at least three peaks, the most unorthodox feature of the emotional structure is the placing of the most sustained and intense of these midway through the story. Le Fanu gets away with putting the climax in the middle by making it a dream sequence, thereby deceiving us into accepting the rest of the plot as factual; the dream is so unpleasant that we accept the ensuing reality—fantastic as it would otherwise seem—almost with relief. Dreams, of course, are a natural for writers of ghostly fiction; even when they do not actually figure in the plot, they function as a subtext, a constant analogy in the reader's mind.

When they do figure in the plot, they serve the useful function of allowing the writer to be unusually explicit in his presentation of the supernatural and the marvelous without causing the reader to renege on his willing suspension of disbelief. This is why Le Fanu can make Harbottle's ghostly trial so extraordinarily detailed and particular; by turning it into a dream, he automatically does away with the basic problem of credibility, a problem which normally prohibits sustained explicitness. In addition, he adds another layer of ambiguity to the story, for we never know for sure whether this is merely a dream. We strongly suspect it to be more than a dream because of what precedes and follows it, but Harbottle does actually fall asleep. Even when Le Fanu distorts the distinction between dream and reality, he does it in a careful, almost reluctant manner.

Since the dreams are based on Le Fanu's own nightmares, they have an exacting authenticity that Le Fanu perhaps could not have managed had he made them up. Dreams have their own special logic and poetry, their own inimitable blend of the ordinary and the magical. Le Fanu's apparition scenes involving wide-awake characters frequently have the same dream-like quality, but the transition to them from an unmistakably "real" context is carefully gauged and often slow-moving. The transit back to reality is desperate, fearful, and—until the last gruesome scene—usually successful. It is as if these stories are afraid to fall asleep because they know they will have nightmares. When they do drop off, they do their best to wake themselves up.

"The Familiar" demonstrates this reticence to a striking degree, both in its pacing and its theme. If "Green Tea" is the most conspicuously modern of the *In A Glass Darkly* tales, "The Familiar" would appear to be the most stodgily Victorian: according to the narrator, even the victim himself "seems to regard" his persecution as merely "working out a retribution for some grievous sin of his past life" (242). But in the end, we feel the same tension between explicable retribution and nameless horror which haunts "Mr. Justice Harbottle."

Reduced to skeletal form, the plot is strikingly similar to "Green Tea." Like Jennings, Sir James Barton is a "saving, prudent, unsocial sort of fellow," "a man of perfect breeding" who is hounded in carefully orchestrated "phases" by an "odious appearance" of supernatural origin until he suffers a predictably gruesome death. There is one difference, however: Barton, unlike Jennings, suffers from an acute sense

of guilt based on a specific act in his past, the nature of
which he guards with Hawthornian secrecy. In an addendum,
we learn Barton's secret. During his career as a naval
commander, he had once formed a "guilty attachment" with
the daughter of a crew member. Upon discovering the affair,
the enraged father had beaten the girl brutally, perhaps
fatally, for "she had died heartbroken" shortly thereafter.
Exercising his authority as commander, Barton had adminis-
tered a similarly lethal punishment to the father, who presumably becomes Barton's supernatural avenger in the
story.

Seen in this context, "The Familiar," with the possible
exception of "The Village Bully," is the closest thing to a
simple revenge tale in the Le Fanu canon. Yet even here,
revenge never becomes a convincing theme; it remains a
mechanical motif in a larger, darker texture of events. In the
course of "an extraordinary conversation" with a "celebrated
preacher," Barton blurts out what appears to be one of the
most extreme persecution fantasies in English fiction. But
Barton's fantasies are like those of Hardy's Jude Fawley;
they are based entirely on reality:

> "The fact is," said Barton, "whatever may be my uncertainty as to
> the authenticity of what we are taught to call revelation, of one
> fact I am deeply and horribly convinced, that there does exist be-
> yond this a spiritual world—a system whose workings are generally
> in mercy hidden from us—a system which may be, and which is
> sometimes, partially and terribly revealed. I am sure—I *know*," con-
> tinued Barton with increasing excitement, "that there is a God—a
> dreadful God—and that retribution follows guilt, in ways the most
> mysterious and stupendous—by agencies the most inexplicable and
> terrific;—there is a spiritual system—great God, how I have been con-
> vinced!—a system malignant, and implacable, and omnipotent, under
> whose persecutions, I am, and have been, suffering the torments of
> the damned!—yes, sir—yes—the fires and frenzy of hell!" (224)

Throughout the speech, there is an incongruous relationship
between the idea of retribution and the way it is carried out.
Since real guilt is involved, the persecution is not as pure or
as diabolically inappropriate as it becomes in the later
"Green Tea." At the same time, the concept of just pun-

ishment is utterly foreign to the worldview of "The Famil-
liar." Although Barton recognizes a "system" in the universe,
he calls it a "malignant" system controlled by a "dreadful"
deity, the workings of which are "in mercy hidden from us."
In short, it is a system which is as secret as Barton's own
crime and infinitely more heinous. In the secrecy, of
course, lies the terror. We can only guess at the extent of
human vulnerability in a cosmos which is at best Manichaean
(with the forces of evil given a decisive edge), at worst
conspiratorial. When Barton complains that he can't pray because "the awful, unutterable idea of eternity and infinity
oppresses and maddens my brain" (226), who can blame
him?

It is significant that at no point does the "celebrated
preacher" dispute Barton's fearful theology. On the contrary,
he seems to confirm Barton's worst fears by implicitly
concurring in this horror vision. On the other hand, he refuses
to credit the particular reality of Barton's pursuer, ascribing
it to the sufferer's deranged imagination, thus leaving Barton
with the feeling of temporary insanity as well as ultimate
doom: " 'My dear sir, this *is* fancy,' said the man of folios;
'you are your own tormentor' " (227). Le Fanu's irony is at
its bluntest here, with Barton, an ardent sceptic, desperately
and unsuccessfully pleading with a pious clergyman to
accept a supernatural occurrence. The clergyman is only one
of the many doctors and preachers who parade impotently
through this and other Le Fanu tales. Barton's medical
doctor, for example, diagnoses his sufferings as "some slight
derangement of the digestion" (218).

The established order loses credibility in other ways as
well. There is the usual prologue, with the usual editor
subjecting us to the tendentious refrain of Hesselius: " 'Had
I seen Mr. Barton, I should have without difficulty referred
those phenomena to their proper disease' "(209). It is difficult to believe this, especially since we never see Hesselius succeed in any of these stories. Hesselius's constant,
belated references to the triumph of medical science strike us
as ironic. The overall effect is to undercut theology as well as

science, for Hesselius merges irresistibly with Barton's
physician and Barton's preacher: both become associated in
our minds with ineffectual orthodoxies and institutions.

The subversion is strengthened by some revealing editorial bickering between the representatives of science and
religion. The editor, for example, criticizes the narrator, the
Reverend Thomas Herbert, for "the occasional stiffness and
redundancy of his sentences" (243), yet seems unaware of
the same faults, much more aggressively displayed, in Hesselius's syntax. Yet the editor has a point in regard to the
Reverend Mr. Herbert's addendum, a document which states
the case for an interpretation of the story in straightforward
terms of sin and expiation. Herbert's case is made in the
vaguest, most unconvincing manner imaginable. Even Barton's "sin" is explicated in such halting, tentative language
that the reader wonders what he has actually committed.
Herbert himself is far from convinced that this interpretation
really explains what happened to Barton:

> Whether these circumstances in reality bear, or not, upon the
> occurrences of Barton's after-life, it is, of course, impossible to say.
> It seems, however, more than probable that they were at least, in his
> own mind, closely associated with them. But however the truth may
> be, as to the origin and motives of this mysterious persecution, there
> can be no doubt that, with respect to the agencies by which it was
> accomplished, absolute and impenetrable mystery is like to prevail
> until the day of doom. (243)

The editor's objections to the narrator's indirect syntax do
not prevent him from preserving the authenticity of Herbert's
original manuscript. He assures us that he "has not altered
one letter of the original text" (243). The lack of editorial
tampering is fortunate, for Herbert is a man who knows how
to tell a ghost story. His tendency toward syntactical padding
and overembellishment is, as the editor admits, only "occasional"; it is also ominously appropriate, given the "dark
and inexplicable outline" with which the narrator is wrest-
ling. The sense of aimlessness, of reluctance to get to the
point, signals the confusion and anxiety of the narrator.
When Herbert does get to the point, when he describes the
shrunken sailor, the giant owl, or the other manifestations

of Barton's pursuer, the scene is all the more chilling for being rendered with such painful reluctance.

This mixture of hesitating indirection and stark precision, the most distinctive characteristics of Le Fanu's prose style, is what makes "The Familiar" so compelling. One is tempted to concur with Ellis's unqualified statement that "for sheer terror, the haunting of the unhappy protagonist of this tale has no equal."[37] Le Fanu was apparently aware of the quality of "The Familiar," for he resurrected it from the obscure *Ghost Stories and Tales of Mystery*, changed the title from "The Watcher" to "The Familiar," and reprinted it in *In A Glass Darkly*. The sense of suffering and persecution in this tale is unrelieved; it is also, as in "Green Tea," carefully modulated, from the dread and near madness of the initial phases to the "apathy of entire despair," "the anticipated stillness of the grave" immediately preceding the climax.

The climax itself, delivered from the point of view of a servant, is a good example of Le Fanu's ability to delineate the form of a ghostly confrontation while only suggesting the content:

> Palsied by a feeling akin to terror, yet not unmingled with curiosity, he stood breathless and listening at the threshold, unable to summon resolution to push open the door and enter. Then came a rustling of the curtains, and a sound like that of one who in a low voice hushes a child to rest, in the midst of which he heard Barton say, in a tone of stifled horror—"Oh, God—oh, my God!" and repeat the same exclamation several times. Then ensued a silence, which again was broken by the same strange soothing sound; and at last there burst forth, in one swelling peal, a yell of agony so appalling and hideous, that, under some impulse of ungovernable horror, the man rushed to the door, and with his whole strength strove to force it open. . . . Yell after yell rang louder and wilder through the chamber, accompanied all the while by the same hushed sounds. Actually freezing with terror, and scarce knowing what he did, the man turned and ran down the passage, wringing his hands in the extremity of horror and irresolution. (240)

Predictably, the two men who finally break the door down discover on the bed the "fearful spectacle" of a bug-eyed corpse, "slunk back as far as the solid panelling would allow." They also discover "a deep indenture as if caused by a heavy pressure, near the foot of the bed" (241). The cause of the indenture remains a mystery, as does the "strange soothing sound" which counterpointed the "swelling peal" of Barton's final agony. The march of events proceeds with tragic inevitability, but through darkness: "These transactions must remain shrouded in their original obscurity" (242).

Here, Le Fanu tacitly acknowledges that· the expiation theme fails to light up this tale. The theme acts as a red herring, frustrating our moral sensibilities while seeming to appease them. Red herrings also turn up in "Carmilla," Le Fanu's sole contribution to the vampire myth.[38] Le Fanu's treatment of vampires is consistent with his usual approach to the supernatural in the late tales. His main concern, as always, is with repetitive cycles of victimization. Unlike the more straightforward vampire tales of Prest, Polidori, and Stoker, "Carmilla" does not have a neat resolution in which evil is banished. The obligatory staking scene is as dramatic and explicitly gruesome as Stoker's but it only ambiguously ends Carmilla's ghostly existence; more important, it fails to contain the larger forces of which she is only a single manifestation. In its open-endedness and irresolution, "Carmilla" looks forward to later vampire tales such as M. R. James's "An Episode of Cathedral History" and de la Mare's "Seatton's Aunt" more than it resembles its nineteenth-century rivals.

The most intriguingly problematic of the late tales, "Carmilla" reveals its full weirdness only after several readings. It raises a variety of dark questions, but seldom directly. The most immediately perplexing question is what actually happens to the vampire. Since Carmilla is not only staked through the heart, but also decapitated, cremated, and scattered onto the current of a river, we can assume that she is efficiently disposed of. But that does not end the matter. Unlike Bram Stoker's Lucy, who attains heavenly release when the stake pierces her heart, Carmilla is denied transcendence. Her former lover leaves behind "a curious paper to prove that the vampire, on its expulsion from its amphibious existence, is projected into a far more horrible life" (338). The nature of this remoter dimension of suffering is not explained. This is an odd variation on the vampire theme, but one thoroughly characteristic of Le Fanu. Since Lucy has been bitten by Dracula, she is obviously more victim than monster; Stoker therefore balances the moral equation by having her otherwise hideous death end in ultimate peace. Attacked in her sleep by an unknown vampire, Carmilla is as much a victim as Lucy, yet Le Fanu denies her salvation, dooming her to "a far more horrible life."

Also left hanging is the question of Carmilla's ghostly retinue: the imposing but "rather pale" woman who claims to be Carmilla's mother, the "hideous black woman" with "gleaming eyes and large white eye-balls," and the "ill-looking pack of men," with faces "so strangely lean, dark and sullen." (286) These figures are more sinister than Carmilla, partly because we glimpse them only for a moment, partly because Carmilla seems in some sense their pawn. Implicitly they remain very much at large at the conclusion of the story, only temporarily thwarted by the staking of Carmilla. The same figures turn up in "The Child Who Went With the Fairies," this time as ghostly kidnappers. Anticipating Lovecraft, Le Fanu works with a personal mythos of seemingly indestructible beings who appear in tale after tale.

Since the narrator, Laura, is one of Carmilla's victims, her final status is also ambiguous. Laura is in the unique position of being the only Le Fanu character who is both the narrator of a tale of pursuit and its object. That she survives the ordeal is also singular and seemingly explains her position as narrator: like Melville's Ishmael, she is the only one who survives to tell the tale. In what form she survives, however, is questionable: according to Baron Vordenburg, the vampire expert who anticipates Stoker's Dr. Van Helsing, Carmilla's victims "almost invariably" develop into vampires. Presumably, Mademoiselle Rheinfeldt, Laura's cousin, will at some point rise from the grave to terrorize the community much as Carmilla did.[39] But Laura is also attacked on a nightly basis and for a longer period of time. Indeed the first attack occurs when she is six years old. How many attacks occur between her childhood and her late adolescent narrative neither she nor her readers know; only the first attacks

"stand out vivid as the isolated pictures of the phantasma-
goria surrounded by darkness" (278). Her doctor tells her she
has recovered from the disease, but anyone who has read
"The Familiar" or "Mr. Justice Harbottle" knows how much
Le Fanu's doctors can be trusted.

Laura herself is not an entirely trustworthy narrator, any
more than Hesselius in "Green Tea." She seems capable of
thoroughly blocking out reality. An example is her blank
reaction to General Spielsdorf's lengthy recounting of the
death of his ward, Mademoiselle Rheinfeldt, at the hands of
the vampire Millarca. The anagram for Carmilla is obvious,
as is the parallelism between the General's account and
Laura's own experience with Carmilla. On some level she
senses the truth: "You may suppose . . . how I felt as I
heard him detail habits and mysterious peculiarities which
were in fact, those of our beautiful guest, Carmilla!" (327).
The pock marks on her neck should be the clincher, yet
she still does not make any connections. She is even "relieved
on hearing the voices of Carmilla and Madame" upon the
completion of the General's horror tale. The general of
course is not at all pleased to see Carmilla. He lets out a
blood-curdling cry and assaults her with a hatchet, to which
Carmilla responds by undergoing "an instantaneous and
horrible transformation" into a wild brute and vanishing into
the air. After all this, Laura still does not comprehend what is
going on. Baron Vordenburg, the ever-helpful vampire expert,
has to explain it to her. Her obtuseness may well be a function
of her surrender to Carmilla's considerable charms, sexual as
well as vampiric.

In any case, we cannot rely on her to diagnose her own
vampirism even if the symptoms are obvious. That she may
well have finally succumbed to the disease is slyly hinted at
in the Prologue: the editor, anxious to reopen the correspondence with Laura commenced by the late Dr. Hesselius, discovers that she has died. The cause of her death is not divul-
ged, but the final sentence of her narration hauntingly
indicates that—at least psychologically —she is far from free of
the plague of vampirism: "It was long before the terror of
recent events subsided; and to this hour the image of Carmilla

returns to memory with ambiguous alternations—sometimes the playful, languid, beautiful girl; sometimes the writhing fiend I saw in the ruined church; and often from a reverie I have started, fancying I heard the light step of Carmilla at the drawing room door" (339). For Le Fanu, this is a singularly chilling and evocative ending, accomplishing through a rendering of inner experience what other tales awkwardly attempt through editorial addenda. As usual, the ending does not end things but suggests the circumference of a diabolical circle. There is no release, either in this life or the next.

In other ways as well, "Carmilla" displays Le Fanu's technique at its most sophisticated. One unusual feature of the story is the luxury of a direct angle of perception: we *see* Carmilla; she is the only supernatural force which Le Fanu allows us to observe directly, in scene after scene. This clarity is necessary if we are to identify Carmilla as both victim and victimizer; though ostensibly the otherworldly pursuer, she is also a typical Le Fanu victim, doomed to unending cycles of agony by seemingly random, meaningless events. It is enormously difficult to use a frontal approach in writing a ghost story. M. R. James was most keenly aware of the risks involved; not one of his demons utters a word or appears for more than an instant. Yet Le Fanu manages to invest Carmilla with the same aura of infernal mystery that we experience from less tangible spectres.

One of the ways he accomplishes this is through the substitution of ghostly eroticism for ghostly indirection. The yoking of sensuality with malignance is of course not unusual: the apparitions in "Schalken the Painter," "The Fortunes of Sir Robert Ardagh," and "Green Tea," among others, conspicuously project both qualities, suggesting the author's abhorrence of physicality more than they build toward a conscious theme. Here, however, sensuality is more than a string of lurid adjectives (though "languid" is used a number of times); it is a powerfully ambivalent experience, a balancing of ecstasy and torment.

According to Nelson Browne, "not the least horrible thing about Carmilla is the strain of Lesbian perversity in her passionate declaration of affection for Laura."[40] This is a crude oversimplification, more revealing of the critic than the story. The evil in the story is not lesbianism, but vampirism. The explicitly lesbian relationship between Carmilla and Laura is at least as appealing as it is perverse, just as Carmilla, like Hawthorne's Beatrice, is as radiantly sensual as she is deadly. If anything, Le Fanu is harsher with heterosexual love.[41] "Carmilla" is the only story in which sensuality does not take on a one-dimensional association with evil.

Ambivalence is the controlling principle throughout the story: pleasure vies with revulsion, love with death. A fractured consciousness reveals itself through persistent balances in the language: Carmilla speaks sadomasochistically of "the rapture of my enormous humiliation," "the rapture of that cruelty which yet is love" (291); like most vampires, she speaks constantly of the sweetness of death, longing for annihilation, yet feverishly clinging to what Yeats called "death-in-life and life-in-death." "Everyone must die and all are happier when they do" is her constant refrain. Perpetually in a state of death, she is capable of extending this unearthly happiness which, because she is not dead at all, is also unearthly suffering.

Laura also uses increasingly ambiguous language. She speaks repeatedly of "a love growing into adoration and also of abhorrence" (292), "a fascination" mingled with "a sense of the horrible" (307). She presents this "paradox" in the specifically sexual content of Carmilla's embraces:

> Sometimes after an hour of apathy, my strange and beautiful companion would take my hand and hold it with a fond pressure, renewed again and again; blushing softly, gazing in my face with languid and burning eyes, and breathing so fast that her dress rose and fell with the tumultuous respiration. It was like the ardour of a lover; it embarrassed me; it was hateful and yet overpowering; and with gloating eyes she drew me to her, and her hot lips travelled along my cheek in kisses; . . .
> "Are we related," I used to ask; "what can you mean by all this?" (292).

The passage is sexy, ominous, and ridiculous all at once. Despite the editor's presentation of Laura's narrative as the work of an "intelligent lady," nothing could be more charac-

teristic of Laura's "intelligence" than the question she puts
to the panting Carmilla. She is easy prey indeed.

Throughout the story, the seduction is described in surprisingly non-euphemistic language. When Laura is bitten on
the neck, she describes the experience in terms of orgasm:
she feels a "peculiar, cold thrill" and a powerful "convulsion"
followed by a "sweet," "narcotic" sensation of "languor"
(307, 308). The language suggests an almost Baudelairean
sensibility, a post-orgasmic stupor which both lovers associate with death. As Laura succumbs to Carmilla's unorthodox
seductions, she increasingly associates sexual surrender with a
surrender to death: "Dim thoughts of death began to open and
an idea that I was slowly sinking took gentle, and, somehow,
not unwelcome possession of me. If it was sad, the tone of
mind which this induced was also sweet. Whatever it might
be, my soul acquiesced in it" (307). When speaking to Laura,
Carmilla makes the same association, but more consciously:
" 'I live in your warm life, and you shall die—die, sweetly
die—into mine. . . . To die as lovers may—to die together, so
that they may live together' " (291, 297). Paradoxically, death
is precisely what Carmilla cannot attain. Like sex, its desir-
ability is vastly increased by its unattainability.

In its blending of lesbianism, sadomasochism, necrophilia,
and vampirism, "Carmilla" seems exotically pornographic.
There is an inherent connection between ghost stories and
pornography in that both attempt to produce an actual physical reaction in the reader. Pornography, however, is an epi-
sodic form, banking everything on a series of isolated scenes
which are not obliged to add up to a convincing whole. In
the ghost story, the whole is always greater than the sum of
its parts; cumulative impact is everything. In "Carmilla,"
Le Fanu's dark, ambiguous eroticism is a means toward
making his vampire seem eerie and mysterious. Once this
end has been accomplished, Le Fanu drops the eroticism
altogether. After the "gloomy triumph" of the doctor's diagnosis, the nightly attacks cease: the remaining third of the
story builds toward the horrifying "ordeal and execution" of
Carmilla.

The other means employed by Le Fanu to counteract our

direct perception of Carmilla are more characteristic: these consist of various transformations, the "ambiguous alter-ations" which constitute the final "image" of doubleness in Laura's consciousness. At one moment, she is a "play-ful, languid beautiful girl," the next a "writhing fiend"; she breathes "tumultuous sighs," then suddenly gazes "with eyes from which all fire, all meaning had flown" (300); at night, she becomes "a sooty-black animal that resembled a monstrous cat," (304) swells "into a great palpitating mass," then thins out as a young girl "in her white nightdress, bathed from her chin to her foot, in one great stain of blood." (308)

All this is not without its comical aspects; "Carmilla" has an exceptionally heavy dose of grotesque humor, even for *In A Glass Darkly*. There are incidents and exchanges as farcical as those in purely comical tales such as "The Ghost and the Bone Setter" and "My Aunt Margaret's Adventure." In one of the better exchanges, a travelling dentist comes closer to the truth than he realizes when he comments on the extraordinary ugliness of Carmilla's teeth. He offers to "blunt" them, but Carmilla sullenly declines the offer. Dramatic irony crops up in many Le Fanu tales, but it becomes endemic here. With the exception of the reader, the cleverly cynical Carmilla is always several jumps ahead of everyone. She delivers her best lines when Laura's father offers to call the doctor to help ward off the strange disease that is wasting the countryside:

"Doctors never did me any good," said Carmilla. "Then you have been ill?" I asked.
"More ill than ever you were," she answered. (297)

These lines can serve as a deadpan summary of the pre-dicament of Le Fanus' characters: doctors never do any of them any good. They are peculiarly helpless—relentlessly har-ried by life, yet unable to attain the release of death. The fantasy of nothingness articulated by Samuel Beckett's Watt could well be Carmilla's fantasy:

Then the gnashing ends, or it goes on, and one is in the pit, in the hollow, the longing for longing gone, the horror of horror, and one is in the hollow, at the foot of all the hills, the ways down, the ways up, and free at last, for an instant free at last, nothing at last.[41]

To be "nothing at last" would be as blissful for Barton, Carmilla, or Harbottle as it would be for Watt or Molloy. But for Le Fanu's doomed heroes, there is no release. For them, the "horror of horror"—the awareness, not only of their suffering, but of its meaninglessness—repeats itself in strange, unremitting cycles. The visionary gallows in "Mr. Justice Harbottle" operates ceaselessly.

Along with gallows, there is much gallows humor. Beckett's "mirthless laughter," the inevitable response to constant encounters with disaster, echoes through these tales with resounding hollowness. Le Fanu's apparitions leer and grin at their victims as if gloating over a private joke. Along with less subtle agonies, Le Fanu's victims must endure the pain of continually missing the point of a grim joke which is being perpetrated on a cosmic level at their expense. On the level of ghost story aesthetics, the purpose behind the "atrocious plan" must remain a mystery. But the crucial point appears to be that there is no point at all. Rose, Carmilla, Jennings, O'Connor, and others seem randomly singled out for destruction, in much the same way as the victim of Shirley Jackson's lottery. If the alien invaders have reasons for what they do, these are kept in the dark. Particularly meaningless are the deaths and permanent insanities of children in various haunted houses: the Tiled House, Applewale House of "Madame Crowl's Ghost," and the lair of the Mysterious Lodger. The persecutions of Barton and Harbottle seem less capricious, but even here the appropriateness is undercut by stubborn ambiguities. These are distinctly modern ghosts, the manifestations of random impulses in the universe. They are apparitions from the void.

This is not to deny that Le Fanu's stories are delightful entertainments: E. F. Benson is probably right when he claims that Le Fanu "produces, page for page, a far higher percentage of terror than the more widely read Edgar Allan Poe."[43] And E. F. Bleiler is harsh but accurate in his judgment that Dickens, Wilkie Collins, Amelia B. Edwards, Rhoda Broughton, Mrs. Riddell, and Le Fanu's other Victorian rivals were too "constricted in technique and ideas" to produce anything like his customary shuddery effects.[44] The intensity and authenticity of horror and agony in the stories suggest, however, that these fictions sprang from a deeper source than a desire to entertain. Whether there existed a one-to-one correspondence between Le Fanu's private vision and the vision of the stories can only be a matter of speculation. It is important that we at least ask the right question: the issue is not whether Le Fanu literally feared ghosts, lesbian vampires, and crawling hands, but whether he feared the abyss from which they materialize, the "malignant system" of which they are only the interrelating parts. In short, did he see the world as a conspiracy?

For Jennings, Barton, and the others to whom this system has been "terribly and partially revealed," no leap of faith is required. They see in a glass darkly, but they do not hallucinate. The darkness is clearly there: if it wells up from within their psyches, it also has its counterpart in the actual world. A real correspondence obtains between mind and matter—as much so as in Wordsworth or Emerson—but an altogether undesirable one. According to Barton, the less we know, either about ourselves or the outer world, the better off we are: the truth is "in mercy, hidden from us." Le Fanu has been called a Romantic and a mystic, but his stories suggest that he was at least as appalled as he was fascinated by the prospect of an enlarged human consciousness. If there is any message at all in these stories, it is that the world—both inner and outer— is inexplicably hostile. The best we can do is keep our distance and hope we never see any glowing red eyes.

CHAPTER III

THE ANTIQUARIAN GHOST STORY:
MONTAGUE RHODES JAMES

"Count Magnus," from M. R. James's *Ghost Stories of an Antiquary*, is haunted not only by its own ghosts, but by the ghost of Sheridan Le Fanu. Mr. Wraxall, the hero of the tale, dooms himself by peering at a terrifying sarcophagus engraving which should have remained unseen and opening an obscure alchemy volume which should have remained closed. By doing these things, he inadvertently summons the author of the alchemy treatise, the dreaded Count Magnus, from the sarcophagus. To make matters worse, he also summons the count's hooded, tentacled companion. Anyone who has read Le Fanu's "Green Tea" knows that such creatures are easier summoned than eluded. Mr. Wraxall flees across the Continent, but his pursuers are always close behind. They arrive at his remote country house in England before he does and wait for him there. Not surprisingly, he is found dead. At the inquest, seven jurors faint at the sight of the body. The verdict is "visitation of God," but the reader knows that he has been visited by something else.

In both incident and vision, "Count Magnus" is darkened by the shadow of Le Fanu. The basic dynamic of the story, the hunt, is symbolized by the sarcophagus engraving:

Among trees, was a man running at full speed, with flying hair and outstretched hands. After him followed a strange form; it would be hard to say whether the artist had intended it for a man, and was unable to give the requisite similitude, or whether it was intentionally

69

made as monstrous as it looked. In view of the skill with which the rest of the drawing was done, Mr. Wraxall felt inclined to adopt the latter idea.[1]

Upon reading this insidiously understated passage, the reader who is familiar with Le Fanu immediately knows two things: that the fleeing figure will soon be Mr. Wraxall himself and that the outcome of the pursuit will be fatal for him. Such a reader will not be surprised by the mysterious illogic of the plot, the absence of any moral connection between the hunter and the hunted. Mr. Wraxall is no Gothic villain or Fatal Man; he is a singularly unremarkable, almost anonymous character. He resembles several Le Fanu characters (especially in "Green Tea" and "Schalken the Painter") in that he is a pure victim, having done nothing amiss other than reading the wrong book and looking at the wrong picture. We are told in an ironic passage that "his besetting fault was clearly that of over-inquisitiveness, possibly a good fault in a traveler, certainly a fault for which this traveler paid dearly in the end" (100). We are not told why he is any more overly inquisitive than James's other antiquaries, many of whom are never pursued. The narrator sums up the problem near the end of the story: "He is expecting a visit from his pursuers— how or when he knows not—and his constant cry is 'What has he done?' and 'Is there no hope?' Doctors, he knows, would call him mad, policemen would laugh at him. The parson is away. What can he do but lock his door and cry to God?" (118). This fragmented summary of Mr. Wraxall's final entries in his journal suggests that the horror of the situation is in the chasm between action and consequence. In the fictional world of Le Fanu and James, one does not have to be a Faust, a Melmoth, or even a Huckleberry Finn to be damned. The strategy of both writers is the same: to make the reader glance nervously around the room and say, "If this could happen to him, it could happen to me."

The style also owes much to Le Fanu. In an odd sense, "Count Magnus" is more in the Le Fanu manner than Le Fanu. James's use of innuendo and indirection is so rigorous that it hides more than it reveals. Le Fanu creates a balance between uneasy vagueness and grisly clarity. But James tilts the balance in favor of the unseen. Tiny, unsettling flashes of clarity emerge from the obscurity, but usually in an indirect context. We are allowed to see the protruding tentacle of one of the robed pursuers, for example—but only in the engraving, not in the actual pursuit. In the most literal sense, these are nameless horrors.

James also follows Le Fanu's example in his use of narrative distance, again transcending his model. Le Fanu separates himself from his material through the use of elaborate, sometimes awkward prologues and epilogues which filter the stories through a series of editors and narrators. Sometimes, as in "Mr. Justice Harbottle," the network of tales within tales results in a narrative fabric of considerable complexity. In "Count Magnus," the narrator is an anonymous editor who has access to the papers Mr. Wraxall was compiling for a travelogue. The story consists of paraphrases and direct quotations from these papers, a device which gives the narrative a strong aura of authenticity. The transitions from one document to the other, occurring organically within the text, are smooth and unobtrusive. They are also strangely impersonal, as if the teller in no way wishes to commit himself to his tale.

James's reticence probably relates as much to personal temperament as to the aesthetic problem of how to write a proper ghost story. It is commonly accepted, largely because of the work of James and Le Fanu, that indirection, ambiguity, and narrative distance are appropriate techniques for ghostly fiction.[2] (Material horror tales, such as Wells's "The Cone" and Alexander Woollcott's "Moonlight Sonata," are another matter.) Supernatural horror is usually more convincing when suggested or evoked than when explicitly documented. But James's understated subtlety is so obsessive, so paradoxically unrestrained that it feels like an inversion of the hyperbole of Poe or Maturin. I find his late work increasingly ambiguous and puzzling, sometimes to the point of almost total mystification. It is as if James is increasingly unwilling to deal with the implications of his stories. What begins as a way of making supernatural horror more potent becomes a way of repressing or avoiding it. Often he appears to be doing both at once, creating a unique chill and tension.

Although he claimed to be merely a follower of Le Fanu, his work has a different feel, despite the obvious similarities in vision and style. Indeed, he unwittingly created his own "school," a surprisingly large accumulation of tales for which James serves as a paradigm. At least two of his more talented admirers, E. G. Swain and R. H. Malden, are far closer to James than James imagined himself to Le Fanu.

James published four volumes of ghost stories during his lifetime (1862-1936): *Ghost Stories of an Antiquary* (1904), *More Ghost Stories* (1911), *A Thin Ghost and Others* (1919), and *A Warning to the Curious* (1925). He was originally a teller, rather than a writer, of ghost stories. His first two stories, "Lost Hearts" and "Canon Alberic's Scrapbook," were written down to be read aloud at an 1897 meeting of the Chitchat Society, a literary gathering which met for "the promotion of rational conversation."[3] The readings were intended to enliven what had become a listless, apathetic (if "rational") group. They must not have been entirely successful, for although the readings continued, the group dissolved in 1897; as James put it, in his typical phraseology, the society "expired of inanition."[4] Nevertheless, the meeting marked the beginning of a yearly ritual in which James would deliver 11 p.m. Christmas readings to friends, first at King's and later at Cambridge. At some of these meetings, James read Le Fanu (with "great relish," according to one of his friends), thus beginning the Le Fanu revival which culminated in James's edition of rare Le Fanu ghost stories.[5] Some of the listeners, like A. C. and E. F. Benson, were connoisseurs of the weird and became ghost story writers themselves. Partly because of their prodding, and partly because James's friend James MacBryde agreed to be his illustrator, James published his first and most famous collection, *Ghost Stories of an Antiquary*. As the prodding continued, so did the other collections, even though MacBryde (who, according to James, was the main reason he decided to publish anything at all), died suddenly before completing the illustrations for *Ghost Stories*. The climax of this curiously reluctant career was the publication of the *Collected Ghost Stories* in 1931. By then, in its review of the collected stories, the *Spectator Literary*

Supplement was able to refer to James as "long" having "been an acknowledged master of his craft."[6]

Other than a lifetime fondness for oldness, James's life demonstrates little direct connection to his fiction. His reputation rests not on his fiction, still relatively unknown, but on his contribution to medieval scholarship (though this situation is rapidly changing).[7] James prepared an estimated fifteen to twenty thousand bibliographic descriptions of medieval manuscripts, as well as the *Apocryphal New Testaments.* Unlike Le Fanu, he did not steep himself in Swedenborg or any other esoteric doctrines, but remained, according to the obituary notice of the British Academy, "a devoted son of the Church of England."[8] Nevertheless, his prodigious scholarly activities provided him with the learned tone and much of the content of his stories. Though largely fabricated, the names of churches, manuscripts, villages, and allusive scholarly minutiae in his stories always sound unerringly authentic. In all outward respects, his life was conservative, the perfect embodiment of a successful post-Victorian man of letters: he was a Fellow of King's College, Provost and Vice-Chancellor at Cambridge, Director of the Fitzwilliam Museum, and finally Provost of Eton. Although Protestant, "he liked a grave and dignified ceremonial." In politics, he was "uninterested but faintly conservative."[9]

James once described the ghost story as an inherently "old-fashioned" form.[10] Yet in the context of his life, the writing of ghost stories seemed eccentric and unorthodox, almost a blemish on an otherwise spotless career. Sir Stephen Gaselee refers with embarrassment to the "pile of 'shockers' in his room."[11] (The "shockers" included, among others, Conan Doyle, Blackwood and, of course, Le Fanu.) Gaselee doesn't like James's "or any other ghost stories," but adds condescendingly that "experts tell me they are among the best of their kind." James's biographer and lifelong friend, S. G. Lubbock, devotes only a single page to the ghost stories.[12]

But the most stubbornly unhelpful commentator on James's fiction is James himself. In his odd preface to his *Collected Ghost Stories,* James states that the only reason he is yielding any commentary at all is that "a preface is demanded by my publishers."[13] Given the demand, the preface "may as well be devoted to answering questions which I have been asked."[14] The answers, to put it mildly, are brief: "First, whether the stories are based on my own experience? To this, the answer is No. . . .Or again, whether they are versions of other people's experiences? No. . . . Other questioners ask if I have any theories as to the writing of ghost stories. None that are worthy of the name or need be repeated here: some thoughts on the subject are in a preface to *Ghosts and Marvels*. . . . Supplementary questions are: Do I believe in ghosts? To which I am prepared to consider evidence and accept it if it satisfies me."[15] This delightful evasiveness represents a consistent effort on James's part to dissociate himself from the clichés which usually dominate discussions of ghost stories. But it also represents an oblique refusal to comment on the craft of ghost story writing (a subject which Edith Wharton, L. P. Hartley, Robert Aickman, and others have always been eager to discuss). The reference to James's supernatural fiction anthology, *Ghosts and Marvels*, is as sneaky and underhanded as any of James's apparitions. If, as James suggests, we search out that rare volume for enlightenment, we find this statement: "Often I have been asked to formulate my views about ghost stories. . . .Never have I been able to find out whether I had any views that could be formulated."[16]

This is more than simple modesty. James's aggressively deflationary attitude toward himself and his material is part of the mystique of his fiction. The stories use every available verbal resource to avoid calling attention to themselves, as if the otherworldly phenomena are creepy enough on their own not to require a loud voice for their exposition.

Moreover, the stories fit thematically into this context, for they often imply a kind of emptiness and restlessness on the part of the characters. It is not "overinquisitiveness" that gets Mr. Wraxall into trouble so much as ennui. James's stories assume a radical breakdown of the work ethic in which the forces of evil take advantage of idleness. Mr. Wraxall is like most of James's heroes in that he is a roving antiquary, a bachelor who is wealthy and cultivated but seems to have no fixed place in society: "He had, it seemed, no settled abode in England, but was a denizen of hotels and boarding houses. It is probable that he entertained the idea of settling down at some future time which never came" (100). Though James does not make much out of the idea, the supernatural in his stories has a way of materializing out of a void in people's lives. In "The Uncommon Prayer Book" (one of his happiest titles), Mr. Davidson spends a week researching the tombs of Leventhorp House because "his nearest relations were enjoying winter sports abroad and the friends who had been kindly anxious to replace them had an infectious complaint in the house" (490). Even those who have a "settled abode" are curiously unsettled.

There is thus an implicit "Waste Land" ambiance to these stories. The characters are antiquaries, not merely because the past enthralls them, but because the present is a near vacuum. They surround themselves with rarefied paraphernalia from the past—engravings, rare books, altars, tombs, coins, and even such things as doll's houses and ancient whistles—seemingly because they cannot connect with anything in the present. The endless process of collecting and arranging gives the characters an illusory sense of order and stability, illusory because it is precisely this process which evokes the demon or the vampire. With the single exception of Mr. Abney in "Lost Hearts," James's men of leisure are not villainous, merely bored. Their adventures represent a sophisticated version of the old warning that idleness is the devil's workshop.

This is a crucial difference between James and Le Fanu. In Le Fanu, supernatural horror is peculiarly militant—it can emerge anytime it pleases. In James's antiquarian tales, horror is ever-present, but it is not actually threatening or lethal until inadvertently invoked. For Le Fanu's characters, reality is inherently dark and deadly; for James's antiquaries, darkness must be sought out through research and discovery.

It is true that the final discovery is always accidental: James's stories are distinctly different from the more visionary stories of Blackwood and Machen, stories with characters who are not bored, but stifled, and who consciously seek out weirdness and horror. Nevertheless, there is a half-conscious sense in which the antiquary knows he may be heading for trouble but persists in what he is doing. An example is Mr. Parkins in the (again) wonderfully titled "Oh, Whistle and I'll Come to You, My Lad," a man whose bed clothes become possessed. Parkins brings this singularly unpleasant fate on himself by digging up a dreadful whistle and having the poor sense to blow it. He doesn't *have* to blow it. He is given ample warning—certainly more than any of Le Fanu's victims ever get—from a Latin inscription on the whistle: "Quis est iste qui venit?" ("Who is this who is coming?") "Well," says Parkins with a nice simplicity, "The best way to find out is evidently to whistle for him" (132).

Another aspect of James which separates him from Le Fanu is the radical economy of his style. Although he hides more than Le Fanu, he etches what he chooses to reveal in brief but telling detail. An example is the apparition (of a man burned at the stake) in "The Rose Garden":

> It was not a mask. It was a face—large, smooth, and pink. She remembers the minute drops of perspiration which were starting from its forehead: she remembers how the jaws were clean-shaven and the eyes shut. She remembers also, and with an accuracy which makes the thought intolerable to her, how the mouth was open and a single tooth appeared below the upper lip. As she looked the face receded into the darkness of the bush. The shelter of the house was gained and the door shut before she collapsed. (206)

Another, more colloquially rendered, is the library apparition in "The Tractate Middoth":

> This time, if you please—ten o'clock in the morning, remember, and as much light as ever you get in those classes, and there was my parson again, back to me, looking at the books on the shelf I wanted. His hat was on the table, and he had a bald head. I waited a second or two looking at him rather particularly. I tell you, he had a very nasty bald head. It looked to me dry, and it looked dusty, and the streaks of hair across it were much less like hair than cobwebs. Well, I made a bit of noise on purpose, coughed and moved my feet. He turned round and let me see his face—which I hadn't seen before. I tell you again, I'm not mistaken. Though, for one reason or another I didn't take in the lower part of his face, I did see the upper part; and it was perfectly dry, and the eyes were very deep-sunk; and over them, from the eyebrows to the cheek-bone, there were *cobwebs*—

thick. Now that closed me up, as they say, and I can't tell you anything more. (217)

Le Fanu would not have cut either scene off as quickly, nor
would he have been as prosaic. Compared to the stateli-
ness of Le Fanu's prose, James's seems spare and unadorn-
ed. Terse and controlled, his stories give the sense of a
ruthless paring down of incidents and characters, a constant editing out of anything which might clutter up the
supernatural experience or the antiquarian setting. But the
scheme is not rigid enough to exclude a frequent light touch,
as the "Tractate Middoth" scene amply demonstrates. Indeed,
the editing itself is often accomplished with droll humor: "Tea
was taken to the accompaniment of a discussion which
golfing persons can imagine for themselves, but which the
conscientious writer has no right to inflict upon any non-golf-
ing persons" ("The Mezzotint," page 40). There is also a frequent impatience with the inevitable stereotypical horror
scene: "Next day Sir Matthew Fell was not downstairs at six
in the morning, as was his custom, nor at seven, nor yet at
eight. Hereupon, the servants went and knocked at his chamber door. I need not prolong the description of their anxious
listenings and renewed batterings on the panels. The door
was opened at last from the outside, and they found their
master dead and black. So much you have guessed" ("The
Ash Tree," page 59). Assuming the reader knows the basics,
James is ever-anxious to move ahead toward his own variations.[17]

This implicit understanding between writer and reader is a
phenomenon common to much post-Le Fanu ghostly fiction.
We know basically what is going to happen, and (if the writer
is reasonably sophisticated) the writer knows that we know:
the interest lies in how he is going to bring it off, in whether
he can play a spooky enough variation on the basic theme to
make us turn up the lights. Thus the concern with technique
in Le Fanu becomes almost an obsession in James, who makes
a programmatic, somewhat artificial use of understatement,
innuendo, and precisely orchestrated crescendo.

But it would be a mistake to think that James is concerned solely with performance. The premises themselves are frequently startling and imaginative. His contribution is to demonstrate that the old forms of supernatural evil are still respectable, still viable, if seen through different glasses. It is as if the reader were looking through the haunted binoculars in "A View from a Hill," watching a familiar landscape transform itself in sinister, ever-changing ways. Vampires, for example, are familiar enough by the twentieth century, but in "An Episode of Cathedral History" James creates a vampire posing as a saintly relic in a fifteenth-century cathedral altar-tomb. The church renovators, surprised at finding a full-length coffin in the altar, are more than surprised when the red-eyed inhabitant of the coffin, annoyed at being disturbed, leaps out in their faces. Witches are also commonplace in fiction, but James's witch (who inhabits "The Ash Tree") has some uniquely unsavory traits, among them the ability to breed gigantic spiders. In all cases, James moves from the traditional concept to his own variation with such swiftness and conciseness that the reader almost forgets he is reading a reworked version of old, sometimes trite material.

On rare occasions, James makes manifesto-like statements about the need for linguistic economy. The Ezra Pound of ghost story writers, James once criticized Poe for his "vagueness"; for his lack of toughness and specific detail; for the "unreal" quality of his prose.[18] The charge is similar to Pound's denigration of Yeats's early poems. Actually, Poe and James were attempting very different things. Poe's tales are not ghostly but surreal. They immerse themselves in the irrational, whereas James's tales only flirt with it. The power of James lies in his ability to set up a barrier between the empirical and the supernatural and then gradually knock it down—to move subtly from the real to the unreal and sometimes back again. The distinction between the two is much more solid than in Poe, where nightmare and reality constantly melt into one another. James's stories assume a strong grounding in empirical reality. In this context, his refusal to accept the existence of ghosts until he encounters "conclusive evidence" is consistent with the attitude of his stories.

The stories are consciously addressed to skeptical readers, readers with a twentieth (or eighteenth) century frame of reference. In making us momentarily accept what we instinctively disbelieve, the burden falls heavily on the language. The way to reach such a reader, James implies, is through clarity and restraint: the hyperbole and verbal effusiveness of the Gothic writers are to be strictly avoided, as are the "trivial and melodramatic" natural explanations of Lord Lytton and the neo-Gothic Victorians.[19] To James, both overwriting and natural explanations in ghost stories are related forms of cheating. Although James usually avoids issuing these anti-Gothic manifestoes, he indirectly pans the Gothic tradition in the introduction to the *Collected Ghost Stories* by refusing to acknowledge any literary debt to it.

To James, only Le Fanu is worth imitating: "He stands absolutely in the first rank as a writer of ghost stories. This is my deliberate verdict, after reading all the supernatural tales I have been able to get hold of. Nobody sets the scene better than he, nobody touches in the effective detail more deftly."[20] Interestingly, James's use of detail is far more selective, small scaled, and particular than Le Fanu's. For all his "deliberateness" and "leisureliness,"[21] Le Fanu's vision frequently opens out onto a large canvas which depicts nameless energies sweeping across the cosmos. The gigantic blob-like entity which hurtles through the trees in "Ultor de Lacy" could not inhabit the cramped world of a James story: there would be no room for it. Instead, such creatures invade the more accomodating outdoor stories of Blackwood and Lovecraft.

In James, even the visionary scenes seem almost prosaic— yet strangely effective for being so. When Parkins, for example, blows his ill-omened whistle, he has the most compact of visions:

> He blew tentatively and stopped suddenly, startled and yet pleased by the note he had elicited. It had a quality of infinite distance in it, and, soft as it was, he somehow felt it must be audible for miles round. It was a sound, too, that seemed to have the power (which many scents possess) of forming pictures in the brain. He saw quite clearly for a moment a vision of a wide, dark expanse at night, with a fresh wind blowing, and in the midst a lonely figure—

how employed, he could not tell. Perhaps he would have seen more
had not the picture been broken by the sudden surge of a gust of
wind against his casement, so sudden that it made him look up, just
in time to see the white glint of a seabird's wing somewhere outside
the dark panes. (132)

If Blackwood had written this passage, he would have used
the "quality of infinite distance" as the tenor for a series of
elaborate visual metaphors, converting sound into several
layers of perception. But James opts for direct images, indeed
a single "picture" seen "quite clearly for a moment." The
combination of momentariness and clarity make for a kind of
ghostly epiphany. Yet though the outlines of the vision are
sharply drawn, the center is obscure. Lonely, anonymous, and
mysteriously threatening, the central figure remains an
enigma throughout the story. We never know who he is (or
what he was)—or why he is so fond of Parkins's whistle.

One exception to James's habitual terseness can be found
in the descriptions of some of his settings. If the present is
lacking, the past is always alive. Whenever James describes
the antiquarian lore which provides the settings for all of his
stories, his prose instantly becomes crowded with historical
or scholarly detail. The opening paragraphs in "Lost
Hearts" and "The Ash Tree" are learned, graceful little essays
on styles of architecture in the early and late eighteenth
centuries as they relate to the houses in the stories. They
provide no "atmosphere," at least not in the Gothic sense
which James so despised, and no ominous forebodings (which
come later). Indeed the narrator of "The Ash Tree" admits
that the entire opening section is a "digression." These
stories are saturated with nostalgia, yet never in a propagan-
distic context. In contrast to the stories of Machen and Blackwood, there are no Yeatsian spokesmen for the glories of the
past. The emptiness of the present and richness of the past
are implied by the distinct absence of the one and overwhelm-
ing presence of the other, but James never forces his fetish
for the old down the reader's throat.

The paradox in James is that this very oldness is invariably
a deadly trap. If antiquarian pursuits provide the only
contact with life, they also provide an immediate contact with

death. Even in tales where there is no dramatic coffin-opening scene, there is always an implicit analogy between digging up an art object and digging up a corpse. In the antiquarian tale, evil is something old, something which should have died. Old books are especially dangerous as talismanic summoners of this evil. The danger is trickier in James than in similar evil-book tales by James's contemporaries in that neither the nature nor titles of the books necessarily betrays their lethal potential. Chambers's *The King in Yellow* Yeats's *Alchemical Rose*, and Lovecraft's *Necronomicon* (all imaginary books) are works with spectacularly demonic histories which the collector in a given story opens at his own risk. But James's collectors are liable to get in trouble by opening almost anything. In "The Uncommon Prayer Book," a remarkable rag-like monstrosity is summoned by a psalm (admittedly a "very savage psalm") in an eighteenth-century prayerbook. For James's antiquaries, even the Holy Scriptures can become a demonic text. Undermining the very thing they celebrate, the plots seem to symbolize, perhaps unconsciously, the futility of the entire antiquarian enterprise.

In a curious way, the style reinforces this contradiction. The most striking aspect of this style, even more striking than its ascetic brevity and clarity, is the gap between tone and story. This gap is especially telling in the more gruesome tales. In "Wailing Well," a small boy is tackled and brought down, much as in a football game, by an entire field of vampires. He is found hanging from a tree with the blood drained from his body, but he later becomes a vampire himself, hiding out with his new friends in a haunted well. (James wrote this cheerful tale for the Eton College troop of Boy Scouts.) More gruesome yet is "Lost Hearts," which tells of an antiquary who, in following an ancient prescription, seeks an "enlightenment of the spiritual faculties" through eating the hearts of young children while they are kept alive. (James is as unsparing of children as Le Fanu.) In the end, the children rise from the grave to wreak a bloody, predictably poetic justice. In both stories, the style is distinguished by a detachment, an urbanity, and a certain amount of Edwardian stuffiness which are entirely at odds with the nastiness of the plots. The narrators

seem determined to maintain good manners, even when presenting material they know to be in irredeemably bad taste.
Alternating between casualness and stiffness, chattiness and
pedantry, James's narrators maintain an almost pathological
distance from the horrors they recount. This contradiction between scholarly reticence and fiendish perversity becomes the
authenticating mark of the antiquarian ghost story. For
James's narrators, sophisticated literary techniques are a form
of exorcism in a world filled with hidden menace. To stare
the menace in the face is unthinkable; to convert it into a
pleasant ghost story is to momentarily banish it. The reader,
however, experiences an inversion of this process: the very
unwillingness of the narrators to face up to implied horrors
makes the stories all the more chilling and convincing.

James disguises unpleasantness in several ingenious ways.
Narrative coolness is one disguise, but he sometimes builds
others directly into the plot. There is a whole class of stories
in which the dark center is enclosed, and occasionally buried,
by several layers of supernatural apparatus. These stories
move toward a gradual uncovering of the layers, but the anticipated climax, the final revelation, is less compelling than
the means of arriving at it. The disguises do not appear in the
form of occult mystification, as in the *Mythologies* of Yeats—
James almost never uses elaborate occult material; nor do they
appear in the form of complex visionary mechanisms, as in the
Georgian fantasies of Dunsany and de la Mare. Like everything in James, the device is disarmingly straightforward
rather than metaphysical. It involves the re-evoking, not of an
actual supernatural being, as in "Count Magnus," but of a
supernatural melodrama from the past. The twist in these
stories is that the art object acts not as a mere catalyst, but
as the substance of the experience. Although the scene itself
is invariably grotesque and horrifying, the interest lies in the
eccentricity of the mode of perception. Moreover, the antiquary is not physically threatened: he is a mortified, though
by no means unwilling, spectator.

James first tried this method in "The Mezzotint" (1904), a
story which became a paradigm not only of several later James
stories, but of several efforts by R. H. Malden and E. G.

Swain.[22] "The Mezzotint" is James's most original creation. In many of his stories, such as "Canon Alberic's Scrapbook" and "Count Magnus," old engravings serve as the prelude to an apparition. Meticulously described, they seem almost to come alive, and they are sometimes more frightening than the spectres they prefigure. In "The Mezzotint," James gives us a picture which really does come alive: the picture itself is the apparition. Initially only a mediocre topographical engraving of a house, it undergoes a series of transformations which are all the more startling for their inexplicability. The collector, Mr. Williams, observes a skeletal, shroudlike figure who mysteriously materializes on the lawn in the mezzotint, crawls into the house and emerges later with a baby in its arms. The final view of the picture is James at his best:

> There was the house, as before, under the waning moon and the drifting clouds. The window that had been open was shut, and the figure was once more on the lawn: but not this time crawling cautiously on hands and knees. Now it was erect and stepping swiftly, with long strides, towards the front of the picture. The moon was behind it, and the black drapery hung down over its face so that only hints of that could be seen, and what was visible made the spectators profoundly thankful that they could see no more than a white dome-like forehead and a few straggling hairs. The head was bent down, and the arms were tightly clasped over an object which could be dimly seen and identified as a child, whether dead or living it was not possible to say. The legs of the appearance alone could be plainly discerned, and they were horribly thin. (50)

The passage is an ideal example of James's art. What we see, we see clearly, as in an etching: what we don't see, we are "profoundly thankful" for not seeing.

There are two layers of supernatural storytelling here: the transformation of the picture and the scene it recreates, itself a supernatural tale. The former is far more mysterious than the latter. The ghost at least has a reason for coming back to life: Williams discovers that the house belonged to an extinct family, the last heir of which "disappeared mysteriously in infancy" shortly after the father had a man hanged for poaching. But the picture has no such reason. Only James could have written a tale at once so sophisticated and so lacking in metaphysical, symbolic, or even causal connections.

His weird pictures are utterly unlike those of his predecessors: the picture of Chief Justice Harbottle in Le Fanu's "An Account of Some Strange Disturbances in Aungier Street" is chilling because it reminds us of the evil Harbottle; that of Hawthorne's Edward Randolph in "Edward Randolph's Portrait" because of its symbolic associations. But James's mezzotint is intrinsically spooky. There is no reason for it to change—it simply does. And to make matters stranger, it never changes again.

We take it for granted in James that art objects are inherently demonic—or at least have the potential for being so. Here we must assume that more mechanical phenomena can be haunted as well. As lean and as calculated as James seems as a writer, he nevertheless possesses the romantic impulse, investing even chemical processes with spiritual powers. Gadgetry and machinery can be as talismanic as art.[23]

Yet James is a closet romantic at best. If we decide that the ghostly power of mezzotints is the theme of the story, we are left with curiously little to say, for James is not interested in expounding romantic or occult theories. The wry, typically understated conclusion discourages the reader from using the story as a brief for any demonic precept:

> The facts were communicated by Williams to Dennistoun, and by him to a mixed company, of which I was one, and the Sadducean Professor of Ophiology another. I am sorry to say that the latter, when asked what he thought of it, only remarked: "Oh, those Bridgeford people will say anything"—a sentiment which met with the reception it deserved.
> I have only to add that the picture is now in the Ashleian Museum; that it has been treated with a view to discovering whether sympathetic ink has been used in it, but without effect; that Mr. Britnell knew nothing of it save that he was sure it was uncommon; and that, though carefully watched, it has never been known to change again. (53)

The brisk parallelism of the syntax in the final paragraph moves us out of the story before we have a chance to speculate on metaphysical ramifications. James's fiction is self-enclosed in that it rarely refers to any system of ideas or values outside the confines of the plot. Mystery writer Gerald

Heard's statement that "the good ghost story must have for its base some clear premise as to the character of human existence—some theological assumption," can refer only to a class of stories (Kipling's are a good example) to which James's are opposed. [24] If there is any theological "premise" in James, it is never developed—and is certainly not "clear." James himself, in the preface to *Ghost Stories of an Antiquary*, is careful to deflate any "exalted" notions of ghost story writing: "The stories themselves do not make any very exalted claim. If any of them succeed in causing their readers to feel pleasantly uncomfortable when walking along a solitary road at nightfall, or sitting over a dying fire in the small hours, my purpose in writing them will have been attained."[25] What is attractive about James's stories is precisely that they succeed in maintaining this weird balance between the pleasant and the uncomfortable.

Other "Mezzotint" stories include "The Rose Garden," "A View From a Hill," and (the most fanciful variation) "The Haunted Doll's House," all of which involve visions within visions which tie themselves into mysterious knots while seeming to unravel. These are the most radically distanced of James's works. In "The Mezzotint," the narrative is a third hand account of a story which itself concerns something never directly experienced. And the character with whom the story is ultimately concerned—the occupant of the house in the mezzotint—is entirely invisible.

Another device James uses to disguise or distance his horrors is humor. Humor and horror, as we have seen in Le Fanu's case, are often two sides of the same coin. Eliot's famous reference to "the alliance of levity and seriousness (by which the seriousness is intensified)" is useful, for James's humor does not defuse horror so much as intensify it by making it manageable and accessible. Without James's deadpan wit, these stories might seem unreal and "Gothic" to a sophisticated reader.

James's use of humor is more conscious, sophisticated, and programmatic than Le Fanu's, whose humor seems more spontaneous (and occasionally unintentional). Often, James will concoct a situation which is inherently funny. An

example is Mr. Somerton's encounter with a toad-like creature in "The Treasure of Abbot Thomas":

> "Well, I felt to the right, and my fingers touched something curved,
> that felt—yes—more or less like a heavy, full thing. There was nothing,
> I must say, to alarm one. I grew bolder, and putting both hands in as
> well as I could, I pulled it to me, and it came. It was heavy, but
> moved more easily than I had expected. As I pulled it towards the
> entrance, my left elbow knocked over and extinguished the candle.
> I got the thing fairly in front of the mouth and began drawing it out.
> Just then Brown gave a sharp ejaculation and ran quickly up the
> steps with the lantern. He will tell you why in a moment. Startled
> as I was, I looked round after him, and saw him stand for a minute
> at the top and then walk away a few yards. Then I heard him call
> softly, 'All right, sir,' and went on pulling out the great bag, in com-
> plete darkness. It hung for an instant on the edge of the hold, then
> slipped forward on my chest, and *put its arms round my neck*. (175)

The jolt we experience on reaching the italics springs as much
from the absurdity of the situation as from the horror: it
scarcely matters whether we shudder or laugh. Ideally, we
should do both.

James frequently entrusts major scenes to colloquial, clown-
ish narrators—usually cockney servants. The servant's account of Mr. Potwitch's death in "The Uncommon Prayerbook" is both ghoulish and comic:

> "And then, sir, I see what looked to be like a great roll of old
> shabby white flannel, about four to five feet high, fall for-ards out
> of the inside of the safe right against Mr. Potwitch's shoulder as he
> was stooping over; and Mr. Potwitch, he raised himself up as it
> were, resting on his hands on the package, and gave a exclamation.
> And I can't hardly expect you should take what I says, but as true
> as I stand here I see this roll had a kind of a face in the upper end
> of it, sir. You can't be more surprised than what I was, I can assure
> you, and I've seen a lot in me time. Yes, I can describe it if you wish
> it, sir; it was very much the same as this wall here in colour (the wall
> had an earth-coloured distemper) and it had a bit of a band tied
> round underneath. And the eyes, well they was dry-like, and much as
> if there was two big spiders' bodies in the holes. Hair? no, I don't
> know as there was much hair to be seen; the flannel-stuff was over
> the top of the 'ead. I'm sure it warn't what it should have been. No,
> I only see it in a flash, but I took it in like a photograft—wish I hadn't.
> Yes, sir, it fell right over on to Mr. Potwitch's shoulder, and this face
> hid in his neck—yes, sir, about where the injury was,—more like a
> ferret going for a rabbit than anythink else." (511)

Though James's rendering of dialect is skillful and idiomatic, he tends to overuse these servant recapitulations of horror scenes. After a while, the cockney narrators—in "A View from a Hill," and "An Episode of Cathedral History," among others—become an annoying mannerism.

In some stories, James's use of humor has little to do with the basic premise, but seems an end in itself. This deliciously sardonic digression in "Wailing Well" could almost have been written by Evelyn Waugh or Roald Dahl:

> The practice, as you know, was to throw a selected lower boy, of suitable dimensions, fully dressed, with his hands and feet tied together, into the deepest part of Cuckoo Weir, and to time the Scout whose turn it was to rescue him. On every occasion when he was entered for this competition, Stanley Judkins was seized, at the critical moment, with a severe fit of cramp, which caused him to roll on the ground and utter alarming cries. This naturally distracted the attention of those present from the boy in the water, and had it not been for the presence of Arthur Wilcox the death-toll would have been a heavy one. As it was, the Lower Master found it necessary to take a firm line and say that the competition must be discontinued. It was in vain that Mr. Beasley Robinson represented to him that in five competitions only four lower boys had actually succumbed. The Lower Master said that he would be the last to interfere in any way with the work of the Scouts; but that three of these boys had been valued members of his choir, and both he and Dr. Ley felt that the inconvenience caused by the losses outweighed the advantages of the competitions. Besides, the correspondence with the parents of these boys had become annoying, and even distressing: they were no longer satisfied with the printed form which he was in the habit of sending out, and more than one of them had actually visited Eton and taken up much of his valuable time with complaints. So the life-saving competition is now a thing of the past. (630)

Although the passage is irrelevant to the plot, it is highly relevant to the relationship of the narrator to his materials. The understated savagery of the humor establishes a context which trivializes the value of life and death, removing the narrator from the suffering and cruelty he is about to recount by allowing him to treat it all as a grim joke.

A more underhanded means that James uses to create distance is deliberate obscurity. Occasionally he moves so far in the direction of mystification that he runs the risk of leaving us completely behind. This device, James's ultimate disguise, occurs with increasing frequency in the later stories. "The Story of a Disappearance and an Appearance," "Two Doctors," "Mr. Humphreys and His Inheritance" and "Rats" read more like dark enigmas than finished works of fiction. The narrators often seem aware of the problematic nature of this material, even to the point of sometimes warning the reader in the opening paragraph. The narrator of "Two Doctors," for example, describes his tale as an incomplete *dossier*, "a riddle in which the supernatural appears to play a part. You must see what you can make of it." (459) James ungraciously provides only the outline of a gruesome tale in which one doctor uses an unexplained supernatural device to do in another. The tale is densely packed with fascinating hints: a rifled mausoleum; a reference to Milton ("Millions of spiritual creatures walk the earth/Unseen both when we wake and when we sleep."); a haunted pillow which enfolds the head of the sleeping victim like a strange cloud; a recurring dream of a gigantic moth chrysalis disclosing "a head covered with a smooth pink skin, which breaking as the creature stirred, showed him his own face in a state of death"(467). Since there are so many ways to piece together the information, the tale becomes more ominous with each reading. The initial reading is curiously empty and frustrating, almost as if James demands that we try again.

Furthermore, he takes it for granted that we know his earlier stories which, for all their nonrational connections, are easier to fathom. The structure of "Two Doctors"—a sketchy presentation of lawyers' documents—is so fragmented that whatever piecing together we do must be based, at least in part, on patterns from *Ghost Stories of an Antiquary*. "Death By the Visitation of God," the surgeon's verdict, makes little sense unless we see it as a reference to the same verdict in the earlier "Count Magnus," a story which has its own stubborn mysteries, but which is clearly a tale of demonic pursuit. Once this connection is made, "Two Doctors" becomes thematically related to a whole class of Le Fanuesque pursuit tales by James: "Count Magnus," "Lost Hearts," "A School Story," "The Tractate Middoth," "Casting the Runes," "The Stalls of Barchester Cathedral," and "The Uncommon

Prayer Book." But seen in isolation, the ending of "Two Doctors" makes almost no sense.

These sly cross references are another indication of the self-referential character of James's fictional world. His narrative posture, at least in the late tales, assumes an audience of connoisseurs, an elect readership which can extrapolate a plot from a sentence. The demands James makes on his readers are somewhat at odds with his determination to present himself as an aggressively "popular" writer whose sole function is to entertain and amuse in as undemanding a way as possible. This is minor fiction to be sure, but fiction which nevertheless succeeds in creating a universe of its own which can be apprehended only through careful, thoughtful reading. Like so much quality ghostly fiction from this period, James's stories fall into the uniquely alienated category of being too controlled and sophisticated for "horror" fans, yet too lightweight for academics. In his relation to twentieth-century culture, James is very much a ghost himself, or very much like his own Mr. Humphreys in "Mr. Humphreys and His Inheritance," a man lost in a haunted maze.

If James is not a major writer, he nevertheless deserves a larger audience than he currently enjoys.[26] His fictional palate is admittedly restricted, even in comparison with other writers of ghostly tales. His stories have considerable power, but only muffled reverberation. He exhibits little of Henry James's psychological probity, none of Poe's Gothic extravagance, none of Yeats's passion—but he delivers a higher percentage of mystery and terror than any of these. If he is merely a sophisticated "popular" writer, content with manipulating surfaces, those very surfaces are potent and suggestive.

James is far more innovative than he pretends to be. In R. H. Malden's preface to *Nine Ghosts*, he reminds us that James "always regarded" Le Fanu as "The Master."[27] Yet Malden also speaks of a distinct James "tradition," implying that James refined, modified, and transgressed Le Fanu's precepts in ways profound enough to set James apart as an original. He brought to the ghost story not only a new antiquarian paradigm of setting and incident, but also a new urbanity, suaveness, and economy. To a contemporary audience, conditioned by the monotonous brutality of so many occult novels and films, James's use of subtlety to evoke ghostly horror is likely to seem as radical and puzzling as ever. Both academics and popular readers tend to associate super-natural horror in fiction with hyperbole, capitals, promis-cuous exclamation marks, and bloated adjectives. Yet the field is crowded with undeservedly obscure writers—L. T. C. Rolt, E. G. Swain, R. H. Malden, Ramsey Campbell, H. R. Wakefield, Russell Kirk, Arthur Gray, Elizabeth Bowen, and Robert Aickman, among many others—who follow James's example.

James also gave the ghost story a new theme. His ghosts materialize not so much from inner darkness or outer conspir-acies as from a kind of antiquarian malaise. Remaining modestly within the confines of popular entertainment, his fiction nevertheless shows how nostalgia has a habit of turn-ing into horror. This is a distinct departure from Poe, where antiquarian pursuits are tied to sensationally deranged psyches such as Roderick Usher's. In James, the antiquaries are stolidly normal, and their ghosts are real. Above all, James's collectors clearly enjoy what they are doing: those who survive these stories would not dream of giving up their arcane pursuits simply because they were almost swallowed up by unearthly presences.

But the real enjoyment is ours. As readers, we can immerse ourselves in the process of discovery without taking any risks. We can even indulge in expecting the worst. Alfred Hitch-cock has often said that terror and suspense grow not out of shock and surprise, but out of thickening inevitability.[29] James, who had already learned this lesson from Le Fanu, is careful to keep us one step ahead of the character so that the dreams and premonitions are as eerie as the apparitions they announce. This is the delightful paradox of James's ghost stories: the more of his stories we read and reread, the more we know what to expect, but that very reservoir of expectations infuses each reading with added menace. The sheer pleasure of these gentlemanly horror tales continually rejuvenates itself.

CHAPTER IV

GHOST STORIES OF OTHER ANTIQUARIES

The publication of M. R. James's *Ghost Stories of an Antiquary* set in motion a spectral procession of tales about confrontations between antiquaries and beguilingly far-fetched horrors: in E. G. Swain's "The Place of Safety," the Vicar of Stoneground Parish is visited at night by an order of gigantic monks from the sixteenth century; in R. H. Malden's "The Dining Room Fireplace," a travelling collector is scared out of his wits by a Dublin fireplace which breathes; in L. P. Hartley's "The Travelling Grave," an antiquary is swallowed up by a mobile grave with teeth; and in Walter de la Mare's "A. B. O.," two antiquaries are pursued by a living abortion. James, a highly civilized man, would undoubtedly not want to be held responsible for all this, and indeed he wasn't. A larger share of the blame would have to be assigned to Le Fanu. As we have seen, the modern ghost story as a strict literary genre originated with his work. James himself fell heavily under Le Fanu's sinister spell. But we have also seen that there are telling differences between Le Fanu and James, and there are enough stories in English fiction with a palpably Jamesian flavor to justify R. H. Malden's mention of a James "tradition." This chapter is a survey of that tradition, examining both the widespread expropriation of James's basic plot, and the more limited emulation of his style.

In 1927, H. P. Lovecraft wrote that James "has developed a distinctive style and method likely to serve as models for an enduring line of disciples."[1] But if James's place in the hierarchy of modern ghostly fiction is secure, his line of

"disciples" is not always easy to trace. Writers who owe a
large debt to James—T. G. Jackson, Arthur Gray, Eleanor
Scott, and A. N. L. Munby, to name a few—are often hardest
of all to track down. An example is Arthur Gray, Master of
Jesus College, who in 1919 published a collection of period
pieces called *Tedious Brief Tales of Granta and Gramarye*.
Only the second adjective in the title is accurate. Gracefully
narrated and generously illustrated, the collection is nevertheless nearly impossible to obtain, even through book auctions in
the most esoteric horror fanzines.

In addition to the exasperating problem of finding the
works, there is also the difficulty of sorting out which writers
are authentically Jamesian. Numerous writers have capita-
lized on James's antiquarian milieu, but most use it as an
erratic motif rather than a definitive thematic texture. E. F.
Benson, R. H. Benson, Walter de la Mare, Russell Kirk,
William F. Harvey, L. T. C. Rolt, and William Hope Hodgson
have all attempted an occasional M. R. James tale.

One of the most memorable examples is de la Mare's
"A. B. O.," a tale which Edward Wagenknecht unearthed from
the *Cornhill Magazine* for Arkham House. Wagenknecht, an
authority on de la Mare, declares that "A. B. O." "seems
rather in the manner of M. R. James."[2] If the double qualification is awkward, it does accurately reflect the way in
which the tale feels its way about in different fictional
worlds, never quite sure of its identity. Like so much British
ghostly fiction, it is both in and out of the James manner.

It certainly begins like James, with two antiquaries digging
up a mouldy box of indeterminable age and origin. That the
box will contain something hideous and alive is guessed quickly by the reader, but not by the characteristically obtuse dig-
gers, who proceed undaunted in spite of several ominous
clues. The remarkable heaviness of the box is one such clue;
the corrosively nauseating odor it emits is another; most sinister of all is a rusty tube-like appendage beginning in the
base of the box, twisting in serpentine patterns under the
earth and somehow connecting above ground with the gnarls
of a yew tree. The inscription on the box, A-B-O, consists of
the first three letters of a word, the remainder of which has

been effaced by time. The box-opening scene, with its revelation of a thin, hairy creature of "monstrous antiquity," is
also vaguely Jamesian:

> When he again set to work upon the chest he prised open the lid
> at the first effort. The scrap of broken steel rang upon the metal
> of the chest. A faint and unpleasant odour became perceptible.
> Dugdale remained in the position the sudden life of the lid had
> given his body, his head bent slightly forward, over the open chest.
> I put one hand upon the side of the chest. My fingers touched a
> little cake of hard stuff. I looked into the chest. I took a step forward
> and looked in. Yellow cotton wool lined the leaden sides and was
> thrust into the interstices of the limbs of the creature which sat with-
> in. I will speak without emotion. I saw a flat malformed skull and
> meagre arms and shoulders clad in coarse fawn hair. I saw a face
> thrown back a little, bearing hideous and ungodly resemblance to the
> human face, its lids heavy blue and closely shut with coarse lashes
> and tangled eyebrows. This I saw, this monstrous antiquity hid in the
> chest which Dugdale and I dug out of the garden. Only one glimpse
> I took at the thing, then Dugdale had replaced the lid, had sat down
> on the floor and was rocking to and fro with hands clasped over
> his knees.[3]

Yet already the analogy with James begins to break down.
The passage is pitched in a different key than James, assaul-
ting the senses and sensibilities in a way James would probably consider to be "Gothic" and excessive. (This, despite
the narrator's pledge to "speak without emotion"). The stylistic influence of Poe, whom de la Mare admired, hangs oppres-
sively in the air.

As is common in such tales, the antiquaries make the very
bad mistake of deciding not to bury the "damnable thing"
until the next day. By then it is too late; the creature escapes
from the box, pursuing the two collectors until "hope is eaten
away by horrors of sleep and a mad longing for sleep."[4] By
the end of the tale, the narrator is headed for madness. His
friend, who sits in the creature's chest reading his Bible,
has already arrived there.

James would probably consider all this to be a bit much.
Though many of his demons seem abortion-like, it would
surely never occur to him to create an actual abortion as the
supernatural pursuer. But that is exactly what de la Mare
does: "The vile consciousness of that thing on its secret

errand prowling within scent never left me—that abortion—A-B-O, abortion; I knew then."[5] This is the first (and hopefully the last) living abortion in fiction. Though it is an early tale, and though it bears a superficial resemblance to James, "A. B. O." is characteristic of de la Mare's bizarre originality. The exotic symbolism of the yew tree with its rusty umbilical cord, pregnant with living death, is quite unlike a James tale.

If anything, the tale is reminiscent of Hawthorne. The content of the symbolism is an obvious example: "There lay the wretched abortion:—it seems to me that this thing is like a pestilent secret sin, which lies hid, festering, weaving snares, befouling the wholesome air, but which, some day, creeps out and goes stalking midst healthy men, a leprous child of the sinner. Ay, and like a sin perhaps of yours and mine."[6] This is clearly the voice and message of Hawthorne—almost a steal from Reverend Hooper's deathbed sermon on "secret sin"—emerging in a new and sinister context. What begins with James is contaminated with Poe and Hawthorne until it bears only a passing resemblance to its ostensible model.

Numerous other tales pay similar homage to James without sacrificing their individuality: de la Mare's later "The Connoisseur" and "The Tree," Harvey's "The Arckedyne Pew," Hartley's "The Travelling Grave," Rolt's "Hawley Bank Foundry," A. C. Benson's "The Slype House," E. F. Benson's "Negotium Perambulans," and Kirk's "What Shadows We Pursue" all in varying degrees have Jamesian settings and story lines. Each is either too allegorical ("The Slype House"), too steeped in personal damnation ("The Arckedyne Pew," "The Connoisseur," "What Shadows We Pursue"), too visionary ("Negotium Perambulans," "The Tree"), or simply too perverse ("The Travelling Grave") to suggest more than a casual influence, a ghostly nod of the head at the James canon. In America, even the Lovecraft circle owes a debt to James's antiquarianism, but Lovecraft's gargantuan Cthulhu creatures, like so many hyperbolic American apparitions, are a far cry from James's more discreet, emaciated horrors.

What distinguishes James above all from many of the

writers who use him as a model is his narrative temperament. The patches of post-Decadence purple prose endemic to so much of this fiction, particularly to Chambers, E. F. Benson, and Lovecraft, are never allowed to blossom in a James tale. An example of what James would not do is this sentence from the opening of Benson's "The Man Who Went Too Far": "Winds whisper in the birches, and sigh among the firs; bees are busy with their redolent labor among the heather, a myriad birds chirp in the green temples of the forest trees, and the voice of the river prattling over stony places, bubbling into pools, chuckling and gulping round corners, gives you the sense that many presences and companions are near at hand."[7] Like James, Benson is attempting to communicate a romantic sense of place. James, however, would probably not subscribe to Benson's animistic point of view, and he certainly would not use the aggressively "poetic" diction which reinforces that kind of vision. Indeed, he would undoubtedly cringe at some of Benson's banalities: there are no chuckling brooks or busy bees in James's work.

Two writers who do bear a close stylistic resemblance to James are H. R. Wakefield (1890-1964) and L. P. Hartley (1895-1972). Their work is marked by the Jamesian combination of tight economy and generous wit. Although luckless antiquaries often appear in their stories, the plots do not remind us of James so much as do the polish of the language and the intricate fusing of the mysterious with the particular.

Wakefield has always been seen as a kind of ghostly explorer of the territory mapped out by James. The most recent association was made by Jaques Barzun and Wendell Taylor in their annotated bibliography of ghost stories.[8] Perhaps the most interesting critical assessment was made by poet-critic John Betjeman, who wrote that "M. R. James is the greatest master of the ghost story. Henry James, Sheridan Le Fanu and H. Russell Wakefield are equal seconds."[9] Wakefield himself has been careful to link himself with M. R. James, calling James's stories "the best ghost stories in the English language."[10] Wakefield also cites James's fictional world as the proper domain for a writer of ghost stories:

"Antiquarian lore, old legends of antique places, old ruins
and enigmas—from such worn stones and hallowed dust
ghostly inspiration is readily breathed."[11]

Even James's strange habit of simultaneously deflating both
the genre and his contribution to it is seen by Wakefield
(at least in his later years) as worthy of emulation. The results
are humorous and sometimes surprisingly brutal:

> Many—perhaps most—people simply *can't read ghost stories*, those
> poor relations of fiction. They'd as soon read binomial theorem
> stories. A large number of strangers have written to me over the
> years to this effect: "Why concern yourself with such inane tripe?
> Why waste a small talent on this bogusness? You're capable of better,
> saner things." I've found that the cult of such tales is confined to a
> small subset of highest brows. They are extremely hypercritical,
> somewhat resembling ballet-maniacs in their encyclopedic knowl-
> edge and zeal for odious comparisons.[12]

Wakefield does not move from here to the expected defense
of the genre: he comments on the decline of interest in supernatural fiction (a situation which has dramatically reversed
itself since he wrote this piece in 1961), but without tears.

The stories themselves, from *They Return at Evening* (1928)
to *Strayers from Sheol* (1961), have a distinctly identifiable
Jamesian flavor. Beginning in a deceptively low key, they
manage, with few words, to work themselves up to a terrific
intensity. For the most part, they shut off abruptly after
the climax; when a denouement does occur, it is extremely
brief. As a member of the generation following James, Wakefield takes up where his model leaves off. Like James in
his later phase, Wakefield creates a maximum of horrific
effects from a minimum of clues, so that our reaction to a
given story depends crucially on how many other Wakefield
stories we have read. After a while we simply accept stories
like "Into Outer Darkness" or "The First Sheaf," even though
the sense of horror they deliver is unbreakably contiguous
with a sense of puzzlement. The stories also convey a quality
of dark wonder which, as in a James story, is so tersely rendered that we almost miss it: "It was strange and lovely, for
the wind had increased to a gale, and yet the great moon
swung through the stars from a cloudless sky. The earth

seemed vehemently alive, and on such a night, thought Camoys, it was easy to realize that one was whirling through the infinite heavens on a lonely ball" (from "The Alley").[13] Instead of doting on this image, as Blackwood or Benson would do, Wakefield begins a new paragraph and moves briskly back to the plot.

It is primarily the language, then, which establishes the continuity with James. The James tradition really has more to do with linguistic toughness than with "antiquarian lore" or "old ruins and enigmas." In itself, such lore is as much the domain of Poe as of James; the difference is in the treatment.

Wakefield's use of language depends on the accumulation of small but telling details. An example is this passage from "Old Man's Beard," the story of a young woman pursued by a ghoulish old man who attempts to smother her with his beard. The participants in the conversation are the victim's father and her newly-hired psychiatrist:

> "What does she hear whispered?" asked Mr. Bickley.
> "She is uncertain about that. She thinks she has heard the words 'September the tenth,' but usually it sounds more like vague chatter. She likened it rather vividly to those soft husky mutterings one often hears between items on the radio. And once or twice she fancies she hears a sort of sniggering chuckle. She believes she heard such a sound first before she felt that tickling sensation."[14]

It is the seemingly innocuous radio analogy (surely as much as the "sniggering chuckle" or the "tickling sensation") which makes this passage so peculiarly horrifying. In recapitulating the stage-by-stage escalation of the horror, the passage reminds us that Le Fanu is the ultimate source for the modern ghost story. By the end of the story, the old man's beard is even attacking the girl when she goes swimming, creeping up her legs from under the water.

Another striking quality of the passage is its tone: the detachment somehow adds an additional dimension of terror to the writing. Wakefield alternates between aloofness and drollery, the last qualities one would expect in fiction which conjures up fear. He can be every bit as witty as James, as another passage from "Old Man's Beard" illustrates:

> The following August she became affianced to a certain Mr. Peter
> Raines, whose past is as bland and innocent as an infant's posterior,
> but concerning whose future stupendous prophecies are made. He has
> just left Oxford, where he was President of the Union, and only the
> fact that he has been adopted as Conservative candidate for a Mid-
> land constituency has prevented him from completing a really "bril-
> liant and daring" novel. As it is, he is about to publish a slim volume
> of essays entitled, *Constructive Toryism*.[15]

As is the case with James, many of Wakefield's most pungent
jibes are at the expense of writers or antiquaries: "The whole
place just suited Lander, who was—or it might be more
accurate to say, wanted to be—a novelist; a commonplace
and ill-advised ambition, but he had money of his own and
could afford to wait" ("The Frontier Guards").[16] The clarity,
wit, and wide-awake skepticism of Wakefield's tone give his
fiction a credibility which seduces the reader into accepting
the most fantastic supernatural phenomena. This is precisely
the strategy which James exploits so winningly and which
contrasts so strikingly with the occultist fiction of Yeats and
the neo-Gothic fiction of Hugh Walpole and Bram Stoker.

The problem with Wakefield is that the sophistication of
his method is sometimes at odds with trite material. He has
a fondness for unabashedly melodramatic story lines and
singlemindedly villainous characters. James is careful to make
his antiquaries neutral and interchangeable so that interest
is focused on the supernatural occurrence. Wakefield's
supernatural concepts are wonderfully imaginative, but our
interest in them is often deflected by gratuitously nasty
characters who scheme and foam at the mouth in the manner
of Vincent Price in a Roger Corman movie. "The Triumph of
Death," "That Dieth Not," "In Collaboration," and "Four
Eyes" are examples of this tendency: they are all supernatural
revenge tales in which the reader is invited to take delight
in the final, gruesome victimization of nefarious victimizers.
In addition to their triteness, revenge tales have the additional weakness of eliminating any sympathy we might feel
for the character. Furthermore, since the character is getting
what he deserves, such tales are always dangerously on the
verge of becoming allegories. As James points out, the ghostly
and the didactic do not mix well.

A related weakness is Wakefield's penchant for violence. James uses violence selectively, but Wakefield, at least in his later tales, dwells upon it pornographically. His pen is deeply immersed in blood. "Four Eyes," which describes what happens when the wrong person wears a pair of haunted glasses (a "dead man's specs") is cruelly typical:

> She went out of the room leaving him standing there. And then it was as if some soundless, piercing power poured through the house. He reeled as it passed him. He heard Bella utter a high, thin scream. He dashed from the room and out into the little backyard. Bella was lying on her face; her arms outstretched.
> "Bella!" he cried. But there was no reply. He bent over and gently turned her body. And then he dropped and jerked back, for her face was a mask of blood and splinters of glass driven hard into it. She had no eyes.
> Old Tarzan, who had followed his master out, moved forward with dragging tail and sniffed at her uncertainly.[17]

Beginning with *The Clock Strikes Twelve* (1946), Wakefield's increasing reliance on violent endings becomes a kind of tiresome, sadistic mannerism. A story like "The Alley" (which has marvelously menacing touches along the way) erupts into such a gory chaos of physical mutilation that the effect is muddled as well as sickening. The addiction to shock endings becomes a trap in which the success or failure of a story is simply a function of whether the shock registers. Bierce's horror tales have the same pitfall, as do more than a few tales by contemporary writers (such as Robert Bloch, Charles Birkin, and Brian Lumley).

Wakefield is at his best when he blends brutality with carefully timed apparitional sequences rather than when he unleashes it in a final assault. An example is "Death of a Poacher," a Le Fanuesque pursuit tale. Barzun and Taylor accurately call this a "stunning" tale;[18] it works because the conclusion is a powerful culmination rather than a shock. Dread and cruelty take on metaphysical qualities, much as they do in Le Fanu. Indeed Sir Willoughby's hyena, a creature "infinitely loathsome and sinister," seems much like a gigantic version of Jennings's monkey in "Green Tea." The spare, businesslike style is closer to James than to Le Fanu, but the tale is a worthy successor to either.

More consistently satisfying are the ghost stories of L. P.
Hartley. Unlike Wakefield and James, Hartley is not a hard-
core specialist in supernatural fiction. The author of *Eustace
and Hilda*, *The Go-Between* and other novels of manners and
morals, he is generally not thought of as a ghost story writer
at all. "Among our contemporary novelists," writes Paul
Bloomfield, "Hartley is the master of sensibility."[19] But an
integral part of Hartley's own sensibility is a keen interest
in the fantastic and the diabolical: "Hartley often introduces
the uncanny into his work, especially into the short stories,
sometimes just to make our flesh creep," sometimes to show
us "that there are times when our psyche projects itself out-
wards in mysterious ways."[20]

Actually, there is no contradiction or even polarity between
these two projects. As Hartley himself points out, the superior flesh-creeper automatically integrates the demonic
with the psychological.[21] Only writers with the most "flex-
ible" and "transforming" imaginations are capable of doing
this.[22] But critics often feel a righteous obligation to concoct
hierarchical distinctions between complementary impulses.
The next step is to declare themselves uninterested in material
that they have assigned to an inferior category. Peter Bien
goes so far as to create a scapegoat for Hartley's ghostly
interests, blaming Cynthia Asquith for his aberrant behavior in
writing ghost stories. According to Bien, it was Lady Cynthia
"who encouraged him to write in the vein of fantasy and the
macabre, and soon began commissioning work from him for
her annual collections of ghost stories. It was therefore
somewhat of an accident that Mr. Hartley produced spine-
tinglers such as 'The Island' and the tales collected in *The
Killing Bottle* (1932), stories which can not, I believe, be considered part of his output as a serious writer. They are a
sideline, and therefore I shall say nothing more about them
(except for a few remarks in Chapter VII on Mr. Hartley's
own attitude toward ghosts)."[23] Actually, Hartley's interest
in weird fiction preceded his work for Lady Cynthia's *Ghost
Book* series. His *Night Fears* appeared in 1924, two years
before the first *Ghost Book*. (Indeed some of the stories in
Night Fears were reprints which had come out earlier in

periodicals.) Included in *Night Fears* was "The Island"; the story was not "commissioned" by Lady Cynthia, and was no more of an "accident" than the other horror stories in the volume. Hartley's supernatural tales span virtually his entire career, as Bien's own bibliography indicates. Far from concurring in the snobbishness of his critics, Hartley declared the ghost story to be "certainly the most exacting form of literary art."[24]

Hartley's ghostly tales deal with every conceivable kind of horror, from the unabashedly supernatural ("Feet Foremost") to the unnaturally natural ("The Killing Bottle"). Part of the enjoyment of reading Hartley is that we are never sure a ghost is actually going to appear in a given tale, yet we are nonetheless assured of a superior jolt. The deftly executed climax of "The Island" (a favorite of Dorothy L. Sayers) is scarcely less riveting then the climax of "A Visitor From Down Under" (a favorite of Lovecraft), even though the former involves the manifestation of an actual corpse rather than a corpse newly returned from the dead. Thus Hartley, like Elizabeth Bowen in *The Cat Jumps* (a collection of ghost stories without ghosts) sometimes violates James's dictum that a ghost story must have a ghost to be worth the telling.

On the other hand, Hartley occasionally sets up expectations of a psychological or material horror story, only to show at the end that the deadly phenomenon was supernatural after all. In "Night Fears," for example, the doomed nightwatchman converses with a spectral figure who appears to be simply himself—the kind of self-destructive alter-ego which Poe called the Imp of the Perverse. Yet after the nightwatchman commits suicide, the mysterious figure is still very much alive; it slinks back into a blind alley, "leaving a track of dark, irregular footprints" and also leaving little doubt of its otherworldly origins.[25] Similarly, by the end of "The Thought," we know all too well that the pursuing creature with the icy breath is more than just a thought.

In all cases, whether or not ghosts are part of the matter, Hartley's stories thrill and horrify because of their manner. Stylistically, he displays a subtlety and power surpassed by no other ghostly writer. Onto everyday settings, he breeds dozens of ominous incremental images which slowly swarm and overwhelm, like cockroaches. To the familiar Jamesian formula, he adds a ringing overtone of childlike fantasy and bedazzlement. His celebrated ability to superimpose a hallucinated childhood world onto the adult world is put to good use in the ghost story, a form which habitually exploits feelings of wonder and powerlessness in a threatening universe. In "A Change of Ownership," the main character speaks of a man who "from a child, had been so ill at ease in his own home that the most familiar objects, a linen-press or a waste-paper basket, had been full of menace for him."[26] It is this ability to see menace in a wastepaper basket that makes Hartley so special. The travelling grave is, after all, only a box, the killing bottle only a bottle, the lift (in "Someone in the Lift") only an elevator. But in Hartley's world, these things are also harbingers of thickly enveloping horror.

If Hartley can transform the familiar into the fantastic, he can also, when necessary, do the reverse. His climactic scenes, many of which are outrageously bizarre, are kept close to the ground of the reader's experience by the use of elemental metaphors that evoke the more fearful moments of childhood. Jimmy Rintoul, the helpless protagonist in "The Killing Bottle," is in bed during one such scene. A butterfly-killer (or "collector," as he euphemistically calls himself), he finds himself ensnared in a bottle-like room maintained by a nature lover who has an exacting sense of justice:

> As, stupified, Jimmy lowered his eyes, they fell upon the screen. It was moving stealthily outwards, toppling into the room. Already he could see a thin strip of the green door. The screen swayed, paused, seemed to hang by a hair. Then, its leaves collapsing inwards upon each other, it fell with a great crash upon the floor. In the opening stood Randolph, fully dressed; he had a revolver in his right hand, and there was a knife between his teeth. It was curved and shining, and he looked as though he were taking a bite out of the new moon.[27]

The entire room is vividly, horribly alive, much like the room in Sir Walter Scott's "The Tapestried Chamber." But the hallucinated moon image could only have been created by Hartley.

Hartley of course is not the only writer of ghost stories who attempts to recapture a childlike sense of the world. According to Peter Penzoldt (elaborating Freud), all writers in the field do this.[28] The difference between Hartley and others who experiment heavily with childhood material (such as Machen and Blackwood) is that Hartley dispenses fantasy in exact, concentrated doses. Though more intense than James, he exercises rigorous Jamesian control. This attempt to place limits on the limitless makes his fiction bristle with tension.

Often a single detail, treated as a creeping motif, brings the unthinkable to consciousness. "A Visitor from Down Under," for example, is literally about cold horror. We know that the visitor is from down under because, in addition to exuding coldness, he sometimes drops icicles from his trouser legs. The device has a striking fairy-tale simplicity. Indeed the entire story reads like a dark, sophisticated fairy-tale. Though the basic idea is simple, the treatment is slippery and complex. The creature is conjured up through an oblique dream-fantasy involving the incantation of progressively disturbing nursery rhymes. As Mr. Rumbold, the pursued protagonist, relaxes in his chair, he envisions a ghostly procession of children, "droning" as they play one of his favorite childhood games, "Oranges and Lemons." After an initial "joyful, carefree promenade," the game changes:

> Mr. Rumbold's feelings underwent a strange revolution. Why couldn't the game continue, all sweetness and sunshine? Why drag in the fatal issue? Let payment be deferred; let the bells go on chiming and never strike the hour. But heedless of Mr. Rumbold's squeamishness, the game went its way.
>
> After the eating comes the reckoning.
>
> > Here is a candle to light you to bed,
> > And here comes a chopper to chop off your head!
> > Chop—chop—chop.
>
> A child screamed and there was silence.
>
> Mr. Rumbold felt quite upset, and great was his relief when, after a few more half-hearted rounds of "Oranges and Lemons," the Voice announced, "Here we come Gathering Nuts and May." At least there was nothing sinister in that. Delicious sylvan scene, comprising in one splendid botanical inexactitude all the charms of winter, spring, and autumn.

Later, the game changes again:

> This time there was an eager ring in the children's voices: two tried antagonists were going to meet: it would be a battle of giants. The chant throbbed into a war cry.
>
> > Who will you have for your Nuts and May,
> > Nuts and May, Nuts and May;
> > Who will you have for your Nuts and May
> > On a cold and frosty morning?
>
> They would have Victor Rumbold for Nuts and May, Victor Rumbold, Victor Rumbold: and from the vindictiveness in their voices they might have meant to have his blood, too.
>
> > And who will you send to fetch him away,
> > Fetch him away, fetch him away:
> > Who will you send to fetch him away
> > On a cold and frosty morning?[29]

Later, Mr. Rumbold is indeed fetched away. The icicles from the "cold and frosty morning" bind the tale together. In one of his most grisly conclusions, Hartley sends a final, icy shiver up our spines:

> The bedroom door was ajar. Putting his head down he rushed in. The brightly lit room was empty. But almost all the movables in it were overturned and the bed was in a frightful mess. The pillow with its five-fold perforation was the first object on which Clutsam noticed bloodstains. Thenceforward he seemed to see them everyhere. But what sickened him and kept him so long from going down to rouse the others was the sight of an icicle on the window sill, a thin claw of ice curved like a Chinaman's nail, with a bit of flesh sticking to it.[30]

Sometimes Hartley's eye for the telling detail is a little sharper than we would like it to be.

His characterization is also unusually sharp. Unlike James's characters, who are virtually interchangeable, Hartley's evince a rich variety of individualizing quirks, mannerisms, guilts, and idiosyncratic neuroses. They are stock characters, but only in a Dickensian sense: they choose bizarre roles for themselves and perpetually act them out until they merge with those roles. Like Dickens's characters, they do this to insulate themselves from reality, reality in this case being boredom as much as pain. James's notion of horror crawling out of ennui, a notion presented but not developed, is given sharp, specific elaboration by Hartley:

> Unlike the majority of men, Jimmy Rintoul enjoyed the hour or so's interval between being called and having breakfast; for it was the only part of the day upon which he imposed an order. From nine-fifteen onwards the day imposed its order on him. The 'bus, the office, the hasty city luncheon; then the office, the 'bus, and the unsatisfactory interval before dinner: such a promising time and yet, do what he would with it, it always seemed to be wasted. If he was going to dine alone at his club, he felt disappointed and neglected; if, as seldom happened, in company, he felt vaguely apprehensive. He expected a good deal from his life, and he never went to bed without the sense of having missed it.[31]

Jimmy's consuming antiquarian interests compensate for his humdrum every day existence. Unfortunately, antiquarianism is a cul-de-sac. "The Travelling Grave" illustrates this point ingeniously: nothing more fully summarizes the futility of antiquarianism than Mr. Munt, a man who literally collects graves. " 'He's one of the exceptions,' " says one of Munt's friends. " 'He's much odder than he seems, whereas most people are more ordinary than they seem.' " Most of Hartley's characters are in the latter category, but they have the unfortunate habit of running into someone (not necessarily someone human) in the former. " 'He really doesn't pose at all,' " says Munt's friend. " 'It's his nature to be like that.' "[32]

In "A Note on Fantasy," Peter Bien categorizes Hartley's characters as being in the tradition of Poe, Hawthorne, and Henry James: "The ghost is not arbitrary, but fits into the moral order of the artist's conception because the viewer deserves to see it, because its appearance is contingent on the viewer's psychological and moral condition."[33] At the very least, this is an exaggeration. Often Hartley's ghosts (and certainly the actions of his ghosts) are indeed arbitrary: "The truth being that she maketh no distinction between persons, but who so admits her, on him doth her vengeance fall. Seven times she hath brought death to Low Threshold Hall; Three, it is true, being members of the family, but the remaining four indifferent Persons, and not connected with them, having in common only this piece of folie, that they, likewise,

let her in" (from "Feet Foremost").[34] This is clearly not the
world of Hawthorne or Henry James, in which the right seers
are neatly matched up with the right visions, the right punish-
ments with the right crimes. Ghost story writer Robert Aickman recently made a statement about "The Travelling Grave"
which is far closer to the truth than Bien's claim of a moral
order:

> But for man standing naked on the disregarding uplands, morals
> are, of course, a cloak, however ragged and patched; and perhaps the
> main reason why "The Travelling Grave" is one of the greatest
> stories in its field, is that it burns up the cloak in a single brimstone
> flash, and travels, if not above good and evil, then certainly far
> beyond them. The reader has a garish vision of all life's elements
> seen for the first time, as in an El Greco. Perhaps it is Satanic. Per-
> haps it is merely the truth.[35]

It is admittedly true that Munt is devoured by his own monster at the end of the story—but only because of a wildly
unlikely accident. This is the bleakly capricious world of
James's "Count Magnus," not a world where horror can be
exorcised by psychology or ethics.

Hartley's ruthlessly cynical sense of humor is another factor
which collapses any possibility of seeing moral affirmation in
his stories. Of all writers of ghost stories, Hartley possesses
the darkest, most consistently brilliant sense of how to mate
humor with horror. His dialogue in particular sparkles with
gruesome hilarity. An example is a passage in "The Travelling Grave" in which Valentine, who mistakenly thinks that
Munt collects perambulators, converses with Munt, who
mistakenly thinks that Valentine knows he collects coffins.
The inadvertent analogies between infants and corpses constitute a virtuoso Hartley performance:

> "They perform at one time or another," said Valentine, enjoying
> himself enormously, "an essential service for us all."
> There was a pause. Then Munt asked—"Where do you generally
> come across them?"
> "Personally I always try to avoid them," said Valentine. "But one
> meets them every day in the street and—and here, of course."
> "Why do you try to avoid them?" asked Munt rather grimly.
> "Since you think about them, and dote upon them, and collect
> them from all corners of the earth, it pains me to have to say it,"

said Valentine with relish, "but I do not care to contemplate lumps of flesh lacking the spirit that makes flesh tolerable. . . ."

"Horrified?" cried Valentine. "I think it a charming taste, so original, so—so human. It ravishes my aesthetic sense; it slightly offends my moral principles."

"I was afraid it might," said Munt.

"I am a great believer in Birth Control," Valentine prattled on. "Every night I burn a candle to Stopes."

Munt looked puzzled. "But then, how can you object?" he began.

Valentine went on without heeding him.

"But of course by making a corner in the things, you *do* discourage the whole business. Being exhibits they have to stand idle, don't they? You keep them empty?"

Bettisher started up in his chair, but Munt held out a pallid hand and murmured in a stifled voice—

"Yes, that is, most of them are."

Valentine clapped his hands in ecstasy.

"But some are not? Oh, but that's too ingenious of you. To think of the darlings lying there quite still, not able to lift a finger, much less scream! A sort of mannequin parade!"

"They certainly seem more complete with an occupant," Munt observed.[36]

The relentless cleverness of Hartley's dialogue makes him a kind of Oscar Wilde of ghost story writers. But as Aickman observes, there is nothing gratuitous about this humor: "In 'The Travelling Grave' we make the discovery that humour is, on the contrary, near the very heart of that synthesizing attitude know as the occult."[37] Hartley's awareness of this synthesis places him firmly in the English tradition which begins with Le Fanu and percolates through James. At the same time, his exploitation of that tradition is so exquisitely personal that it would be impossible to mistake one of Hartley's stories for James's.

Such is not the case with R. H. Malden and E. G. Swain. James's closest disciples, they are the only writers whose stories are strictly and consistently in the James manner. They are perhaps the most obscure of all English ghost story writers. The obscurity is teasingly appropriate, for Malden's *Nine Ghosts* and Swain's *The Stoneground Ghost Tales* are so rare that they resemble some of the much sought after antiquarian occult volumes in James's stories. Also appropriate are the affectionate dedications to James. (Both were friends of James and shared his interest in church history and architecture.) With accurate modesty, Malden calls *Nine Ghosts* "a tribute to his memory, if not comparable with his work,"[38] while Swain, with somewhat less justification, calls James "the indulgent parent of such tastes as these pages indicate."[39]

Both works are so unremittingly Jamesian that reading them almost gives the reader the pleasant illusion of having discovered some unknown James stories. The witty conversations, the detached tone, the arcane allusions, the facetious pedantry, the stylistic economy, the vague sense of ennui, and the interchangeability of antiquarian characters all echo James with an exact resonance. Both writers seem determined to emulate James's every mannerism. Even the plots are often variations on James's ideas, sometimes departing only marginally from the original theme (e.g., Swain's "The Man with the Roller" and Malden's "The Thirteenth Tree" in relation to "The Mezzotint.")

The one Jamesian quality that Swain and Malden strikingly lack (if indeed this is a lack) is a sense of the gruesome. Compared to James, their tales seem curiously non-violent, haunting but rarely horrifying. What makes James so memorable is his ability to disguise horror, only to remove the disguise in oblique, tantalizing ways. He once wrote that the purpose of his stories was to make the reader feel "pleasantly uncomfortable."[40] Whereas James would probably place emphasis on the adjective, Malden and Swain would place it on the adverb.

In the case of *Nine Ghosts*, this reticence is sometimes debilitating. Not only are the reactions of the antiquaries to their accidentally summoned ghosts excessively bemused and casual, but the ghosts themselves are introduced too matter-of-factly. Part of the problem lies in Malden's style, which is efficient but not especially distinguished. The very absence of physical dread in "A Collector's Company," "The Coxwain of the Lifeboat," and "The Priest's Brass" places a greater burden on verbal nuance to make the ghosts convincing in more subtle ways. Lacking linguistic subtlety, Malden relies artificially on Jamesian disguise, sometimes pushing it to an impotent extreme: "I could see nothing of his face, for which

I was thankful. There was something indescribably sinister, worse than sinister, downright evil about him."[41] Instead of part of the face, as we would get in James, we get no face at all. What we are left with are vague generalizations: "indescribably sinister," "downright evil." A ghost story without a furtive glimpse of an evil face is like a detective story without a crime. We feel cheated.

Yet *Nine Ghosts* is not without its strengths. The very simplicity and literalism of Malden's diction often deliver surprisingly forceful effects. An example is this description of a priest being pursued by what appear to be demonic counterparts to the Israelites in their march through the Red Sea:

> At first I should have said there were thirty or forty in the party, but when they had drawn a little nearer they seemed to be not more than ten or a dozen strong. A moment later I saw to my surprise that they were reduced to five or six. The advancing figures seemed to be melting into one another, something after the fashion of dissolving views. Their speed and stature increased as their numbers diminished, suggesting that the survivors had, in some horrible fashion, absorbed the personality of their companions. Now there appeared to be only three, then one solitary figure of gigantic stature rushing down the grove towards me at a fearful pace, without a sound. As he came the mist closed behind him, so that his dark figure was thrown up against a solid background of white: much as mountain climbers are said sometimes to see their own shadows upon a bank or cloud. On and on he came, until at last he towered above me and I saw his face. It has come to me once or twice since in troubled dreams, and may come again. But I am thankful that I have never had any clear picture of it in my waking moments. If I had I should be afraid for my reason. I know that the impression which it produced upon me was that of intense malignity long baffled, and now at last within reach of its desire. I believe I screamed aloud. Then after a pause, which seemed to last for hours, he broke over me like a wave. There was a rushing and a streaming all round me, and I struck out with my hands as if I were swimming. The sensation was not unlike that of rising from a deep dive: there was the same feeling of pressure and suffocation, but in this case coupled with the most intense physical loathing. The only comparison which I can suggest is that I felt as a man might feel if he were buried under a heap of worms or toads.[42]

The passage is strongly reminiscent of James, especially in the use of simple, "unpoetic" analogies instead of real metaphors. The passage also illustrates Malden's superior conceptual powers: his plots are always strong, even when the execution is disappointing. It scarcely matters that the premises are so unrepentantly similar to James's; that is part of their charm.

If *Nine Ghosts* is erratically delightful, *The Stoneground Ghost Tales* is persistently so. In the first place, Swain's Reverend Roland Batchel, vicar of Stoneground parish, is a winning creation. Intractably conservative, he is the perfect antiquary, a man who collects and arranges relics and artifacts, partly out of a worship for the past, partly out of a need to create the illusion that nothing is ever out of its place: "There was a light wind blowing, and the sounds in the library were more than usually suggestive of a person moving about. He almost determined to have the sashes 'seen to,' although he could seldom be induced to have anything 'seen to.' He disliked changes, even for the better, and would submit to great inconvenience rather than have things altered with which he had become familiar."[43]

James's collectors are much the same way, but we never get to know any one of them as well as we do Batchel. For Batchel appears in all of the Stoneground tales, and he encounters in that haunted parish some of the most memorable ghosts in fiction. The "creamy vaporous figure" who materializes in the eastern window of the church; the man with the "indescribably horrible suffering face, rolling the lawn with a large roller" in a supernaturally animated photograph; the ghost who harasses Batchel into reburying his misplaced bone in consecrated ground; the "tonsured giant" who aids, then betrays Batchel in his search for some rare sixteenth-century candle censers; the vampire with the iron bludgeon whom Batchel accidentally unleashes by digging up the creature's stake and chain; and the charming young Lubrietta, whose soul leaves her body during an exam trauma to regrade the paper that Batchel has unmercifully failed—all have lasting poetic resonance. Unlike James's ghosts, not all of Swain's are malignant. One of them, the fetching Lubrietta (who is actually a ghost for only part of the story), addresses Batchel in a letter as " 'dear one.' " Batchel "knows well enough that such terms as 'dear one' are addressed to bald gentlemen only in a Pickwickian sense," but nevertheless "he presumptuously calls" her husband " 'the other fellow'."[44] Swain does not limit himself to James's prescription that ghosts in fiction are obliged to be unpleasant.

As these passages suggest, Swain possesses a style of considerable wit and pungency. If not as original, he is every bit as refined as James. It is unfortunate that *The Stoneground Ghost Tales* must be given the tiresome label of "neglected masterpiece" rather than simply called a masterpiece. There is a gracefulness, even a gentleness, about Swain's ghostly scenes that does not impinge upon their capacity to chill:

> There were other times also, at which Mr. Batchel would use the books. Not being a sound sleeper (for book-loving men seldom are), he elected to use as a bedroom one of the two chambers which opened at either side into the library. The arrangement enabled him to beguile many a sleepless hour amongst the books, and in view of these nocturnal visits he kept a candle standing in a sconce above the desk, and matches always ready to his hand. . . .
> The moon, by this time, had passed out of the south, and the library seemed all the darker by contrast with the moonlit chamber he had left. He could see nothing but two blue-grey rectangles formed by the windows against the sky, the furniture of the room being altogether invisible. Groping along to where the table stood, Mr. Batchel felt over its surface for the matches which usually lay there; he found, however, that the table was cleared of everything. He raised his right hand, therefore, in order to feel his way to a shelf where the matches were sometimes mislaid, and at that moment, whilst his hand was in mid-air, the matchbox was gently put into it![45]

It is this delicate texture of spookiness which gives Swain a voice of his own. Though James is obviously his model, he paints with individual strokes while pretending to merely photograph.

The results are analogous to what happens in James's "The Mezzotint." The analogy holds for all the writers and individual stories we have examined in this chapter, though in richly varying degrees: a given story will look more or less like a photograph of a James story, with the same attractive house or church, the same tidy lawn—until something mysteriously out of place appears on that lawn and begins to skulk about on its own.

CHAPTER V

THE VISIONARY GHOST STORY:
ALGERNON BLACKWOOD

Algernon Blackwood's "The Transfer" is perhaps the strangest of all vampire tales. The vampire is not a demon, a corpse, a bat, or even a rapacious Wellsian plant. Rather, the vampire is an ugly, barren, somehow "hungry" patch of earth: "In contrast to the rich luxuriance of the whole amazing garden it was like a glimpse of death amid life, a centre of disease that cried for healing lest it spread."[1] Jamie, the little boy who feeds it dead birds and mice, is the only one who understands it: " 'It's hungry, don't you see? But I know what would make it feel all right.' " (231). What would make it feel all right is, of course, a human being. The victim, Mr. Frene, is ideal. Metaphorically, he is a kind of vampire himself, a man whose "eyes and voice and presence devitalised you" (233), "a great human sponge, crammed and soaked with the life, or proceeds of life, absorbed from others—stolen" (234). Bloated with life and energy, he makes a more than satisfactory meal for the starving patch of earth when he is psychically swallowed up at the end. The ending is a happy one, at least for the patch of earth: "It lay untouched, full of great, luscious driving weeds and creepers, very strong, full-fed and bursting with life" (239).

"The Transfer" represents a movement out of the claustrophobic world of old houses, churches, and mausoleums into the cosmic world of outdoor ghost stories, a world where ghosts and demons are apparitions of primal forces in nature. The patch of earth is the "emissary" of an unseen life-force

112

which can be glimpsed only through constant experiments in metaphor: "It was like a gulp; it was deep and muffled and it dipped way into the earth. Again I thought of a troop of small black horses galloping away down a subterranean passage beneath my feet—plunging into the depths—their trampling growing fainter and fainter into buried distance" (238). The language alone tells us that the narrator is not a stuffy Jamesian antiquary who is only in touch with books. This is the language of a visionary who is in touch with a living universe.

It would be schematically easy simply to classify Blackwood as the master of the outdoor ghost story; he not only wrote more of them than anyone else, but he managed to create at least two authentic masterpieces, "The Willows" and "The Wendigo." But Blackwood also wrote more than a few claustrophobic haunted house tales, some of them (such as "The Listener") worthy to stand beside Le Fanu's "Strange Disturbances in Aungier Street" and Wakefield's "Blind Man's Buff." In addition, he wrote intermediary tales such as "A Haunted Island" which move in and out between the freedom of nature and the oppressiveness of old houses.

What binds Blackwood's work together is not a common setting, but a distinctive use of language and a distinctive vision. The vision is peculiar in that it is announced decisively but is undermined by the structure of the stories until it seems strangely unsure of itself. This ambivalence adds tension and intellectual credibility to the stories, which would be impossibly dull were they as programmatically "mystical" as they pretend to be.

Unlike the mundane characters of Le Fanu and James, Blackwood's heroes are visionaries who feel oppressed by everyday reality and who deliberately seek out other worlds. What they discover usually encompasses both ecstasy and horror, though sometimes only horror. In either case, the "other" reality is as unmanageable as the first, and the character often spends the rest of the tale desperately negotiating a reentrance into what was renounced in the first place. Rarely, however, is there the slightest verbal retraction of the initial renunciation. Because most of Blackwood's heroes do make it back, he has been seen to be an uncharacteristically "positive"

writer for this genre.[2] There are few upbeat endings in Wakefield, M. R. James, or Hartley, and almost none in Le Fanu.
On the other hand, Blackwood's characters, while they live to
tell the tale, usually end where they started; the stories read
like unresolved circles.

Blackwood's fiction is part of an intensively subjectivist
tendency in modern British fiction. Reacting against Victorian scientism and technology, his characters are constantly
indicting the outer world and plunging into inner vision. As we
have seen, M. R. James also expresses an alienation from the
modern world, but more through implication than authorial
statement. Blackwood belongs to a more didactic tradition of
ghost story writers which includes Yeats, Arthur Machen, Oliver Onions, E. F. Benson, and (somewhat ambiguously) Walter de la Mare. The writers in this group are quite individual,
but they do have a few things in common. One is an earnest-
ness of tone, an unease with irony, a desire to be taken with
intense seriousness. For this reason, Walter de la Mare—even
though his stories are permeated with rarefied visions—does
not fit comfortably in this visionary company. His tone has
too much fluidity, too much capacity for irony and conscious
self-parody. Nevertheless, de la Mare's meticulously crafted
stories do express the common desire of these writers to be rid
of the modern world. In Machen's "The Great God Pan" and
"The Inmost Light," the desire creates a sense of strain, a tendency toward stagey exposition and heavy-handed occultist
dialogue. But Machen is redeemed by his empathy with the
outdoors, his ability to make landscapes come alive with singing prose. "The White People," his masterpiece, has an almost
trance-like lyricism and spontaneity: "I had seen something
very amazing and very lovely, and I knew a story, and if I had
really seen it, and not made it up out of the dark, and the
black bough, and the bright shining that was mounting up to
the sky from over the great round hill, but had really seen it
in truth, then there were all kinds of wonderful and lovely and
terrible things to think of, so I longed and trembled, and I
burned and got cold."[3] As is always the case with Machen's
best work, beauty and horror ring out at precisely the same
moment.

Benson strikes a similar dissonance in "The Man who Went too Far" and other nature stories, but within a consonant framework that allows for the comfort and balance of human relationships. Benson's descriptive prose is also more conventional than Machen's—less magical and surreal, more inclined toward standard late-romantic nature tropes. Though not a very sophisticated stylist, Benson has a sneaky way with contrast: his stories have a healthy out-of-doors quality, an aggressive prettiness, that suddenly becomes stained with the onslaught of vampires ("Mrs. Amworth"), giant slugs ("Caterpillars"), or mummies ("Monkeys"). Gruesome and horrifying in an abrupt modulation at the end, Onions's "The Beckoning Fair One" works the same way.

The visionary writers are not as cohesively linked as the antiquaries of the M. R. James school. Different in style, characterization, and setting, they resemble each other only in their pushy tone, their obsession with subjectivism, and their bitterness toward the grayness and ugliness of the modern world. Blackwood comes closest to being representative of this impulse in that he is thematically consistent (Benson and Onions are not) and remarkably prolific.

Indeed, Blackwood is probably the most prolific of all ghost story writers. During his long life (1869-1951), he published twelve collections of ghost stories and several forgotten fantasy novels. He seemed to possess an endlessly fertile imagination, creating more conceptual variations than any of his rivals. Though his fiction lacks the unity of Machen, Chambers, or Lovecraft (writers who use a central, organizing mythos), it has far greater variety. Like Poe's Roderick Usher, who speaks of "the sentience of all vegetable matter," Blackwood envisions a world in which everything is alive and anything can be a ghost: trees, bushes, earth, snow, even the wind (which in "The Wendigo" becomes one of his most unusual demons). His indoor apparitions are also nicely varied: the old gentleman from the eighteenth century in "The Other Wing," who has a gracious smile and impeccable manners; the leprous thing in "The Listener," who has very poor manners, leaving putrid odors wherever he appears; the Satan figure in "Secret Worship," who appears in a haunted monastery; the emaciated spectre in "Keeping His Promise," who, having starved himself to death, returns to haunt a kitchen, stuffing himself with endless amounts of food. Though Blackwood's human characters behave in predictable patterns, his ghostly characters do not.

Unlike his admirers, who view his work with a kind of religious awe[4], Blackwood is not unaware of the element of farce in these stories. His characters are often tuned into it as well: the narrator of "With Intent to Steal" speaks of the "element of the ludicrous" in the ghostly experience, an element which produces "empty laughter."[5] Laughter is empty because it attempts, unsuccessfully, to exorcise the absurdly grim situation which provoked it in the first place (in this case, the situation of being trapped in an old barn with a ghost whose sole function is inducing people to commit suicide). Blackwood's humor is more closely akin to Le Fanu than to M. R. James. Lacking James's understated wit, Blackwood relies on outright farce. The grotesque silliness of "The Strange Adventures of a Private Secretary in New York" is a case in point. Mr. Garvey (who turns out to be a werewolf) explains why his Igor-like servant so often disappears:

"He has a horrible predilection for vacuums," Garvey went on presently in a still lower voice and thrusting his face farther forward under the lamp.
"Vacuums!" exclaimed the secretary in spite of himself. "What in the world do you mean?"
"What I say of course. He's always tumbling into them, so that I can't find him or get at him. He hides there for hours at a time, and for the life of me I can't make out what he does there."[6]

Given Mr. Garvey's habit of turning into a famished wolf, his servant's "predilection for vacuums" is not altogether surprising.

Blackwood's contribution to the ghost story did not go entirely unrecognized. Derek Hudson has pointed out that several of Blackwood's collections—*The Empty House, John Silence, The Human Chord, The Centaur, Jimbo,* and *The Education of Uncle Paul,*—received highly favorable reviews when they first appeared. E. F. Bleiler, editor of the *Checklist of Fantastic Literature,* recently made this summary evaluation: "With the work of Blackwood, it seems safe to say, the ghost story was finally recognized as a legitimate, respectable literary form."[8] This is an exaggeration, ignoring as it does the civilizing, "legitimizing" influence of M. R. James (to say nothing of Henry James). It also fails to note that Blackwood's audience, though enthusiastic, was always small. According to Hudson, Blackwood himself felt a keen sense of disappointment at not reaching a larger readership.[9]

Blackwood's life resembles Le Fanu's in that it neatly parallels his work. He was very much like the mystical but vigorously active persona in his fiction. Though he returned to England in his old age to narrate ghost stories for the B. B. C., he spent most of his years attempting to live the life of the archetypal lone wanderer, continually seeking new places, experiences, and visions. He rebelled against his ruling-class parents (Sir Arthur Blackwood and the dowager duchess of Manchester) by steeping himself in occultism, eventually branching out into Buddhism and Rosecrucianism. In contrast to Yeats, with whom he became acquainted during their membership in the Order of the Golden Dawn, his rebellion was against Calvinism rather than atheism. He was educated in the Black Forest (which became, in "The Willows," his most memorable setting) at the Moravian school and later at the University of Edinburgh. His parents sent him away to Canada as a young man (where he again assimilated one of his more convincing settings, this time for "The Wendigo"), but he moved to New York, where he sustained a period of poverty later recounted in *Episodes Before Thirty*. Even after fleeing New York, he did not settle down, but alternated between England and Switzerland. Among other occupations, he worked as a businessman, a bartender, a journalist, a model, a milk-farmer, and a private secretary. Like the campers in "The Camp of the Dog," his life was apparently a consistent attempt to "shed" the "disguises required by the conventions of civilization."[10] He never married and was considered "fundamentally solitary" by his friends, who also assert that "he was a happy man and the best of company."[11] Even when renouncing convention, he displayed none of the spectacularly neurotic inwardness of Le Fanu or Lovecraft.

Unlike these writers (and M. R. James as well), Blackwood was a committed believer in psychic experience and ghostly phenomena. At the same time, he shares their refusal to tie any of his stories to actual ghostly experiences. His autobiographical *Episodes Before Thirty* records not a single ghostly encounter. In the introduction to a 1938 collection of tales, he even attributes the muse of his stories to the purely psychological impact of his dreary, poverty-ridden years in New York.

He also seems embarrassed in this introduction, much like M. R. James, by his role as a ghost story writer, though the embarrassment assumes a more elaborate form:

> Yet this alleged interest in ghosts I should more accurately define as an interest in the Extension of Human Faculty. To be known as the "ghost man" is almost a derogatory classification, and here at last I may perhaps refute it. My interest in psychic matters has always been the interest in questions of extended or expanded consciousness. If a ghost is seen, what is it interests me less than what sees it? Do we possess faculties which, under exceptional stimulus, register beyond the normal gamut of seeing, hearing, feeling? That such faculties may exist in the human being and occasionally manifest is where my interest has always lain. . . . Thus in most of these stories there is usually an average man who, either through a flash of terror or beauty, becomes stimulated into extra-sensory experience. A wide gap may lie between a commonplace mind that became clairvoyant and clairaudient from a flash of terror in *The Empty House* to the Man in the Street in *The Centaur* whose sense of beauty blazed into a realisation of the planetary bodies as superhuman entities, but the principle is the same: both experienced an expansion of normal consciousness. And this, I submit, travels a little further than the manufacture of the homespun "ghost-story."[12]

The content of this passage is enunciated with countless variations by Blackwood's psychic detective, John Silence. It is not unlike the prologues of Le Fanu's Dr. Hesselius, the prototype of Dr. Silence. In place of Hesselius's unorthodox medical terminology, Blackwood indulges in the "expanded consciousness" rhetoric of the Order of the Golden Dawn (a rhetoric which is again very much in vogue). The impulse, however, is the same: to transcend the "homespun 'ghost story'" by subjecting the supernatural to the rigors of a quasi-scientific discipline. The desire to have it both ways—to be both mystical and scientific—is characteristic of much of the supernatural fiction of the late Victorian and Edwardian periods, especially in such works as Lord Lytton's "The House and the Brain," Hodgson's *Carnacki the Ghost Finder* (another long-winded psychic detective), Wells's "The Crystal Egg," and Machen's "The Great God Pan." In Blackwood's case, the desire is symptomatic of a thematic ambivalence which sometimes undermines his style. Although the works of his contemporaries are self-sabotaging in much the same way (Wells being a notable exception), the problem is easiest to see in Blackwood in that the felicities and flaws in his style exist in almost manic relation to each other.

Le Fanu, as we have seen, deftly avoids the problem. One of the pleasures of Le Fanu is the deceptive way he has of beginning with Hesselius's contorted proclamations and then going on to write a good, gruesome ghost yarn. The stories come off because the creative impulse is stronger than the didactic.

But in Blackwood, the two impulses are continually at war. At his worst, he is guilty of "a too free use of the trade jargon of modern occultism," a charge levelled by an astute H. P. Lovecraft in 1927.[13] John Silence's endless disquisition on the "etheric Body of Desire" in the otherwise compelling "The Camp of the Dog" is a particularly wearisome example. Whenever the good psychic doctor appears on the scene, we can expect some heavy going. We suspect that Dr. Silence can indeed "conquer even the devils of outer space" (81)—by boring them into a catatonic state.

But even the private moments of mystical awakening by the Man in the Street are often marred, not only by the "diffuseness" cited by Lovecraft, but by a tendency to be too literal:

> It came oddly upon me—prosaic, matter-of-fact, materialistic doctor that I was—this realisation that the world about me had somehow stirred into life; oddly, I say, because Nature to me had always been merely a more or less definite arrangement of measurement, weight and colour, and this new presentation of it was utterly foreign to my temperament. A valley to me was always a valley; a hill, merely a hill; a field, so many acres of flat surface, grass or ploughed, drained well or drained ill; whereas now, with startling vividness, came the strange, haunting idea that after all they could be something that lay concealed within something alive. In a word,

that the poetic sense I had always rather sneered at in others, or
explained away with some shallow physiological label, had apparently suddenly opened up in myself without any obvious cause.[14]

There is something consummately unpoetic about this "poetic
sense." Blackwood is clearly part of the "moment" tradition
in modern British fiction, but his moments seldom amount
to much. Rather than evoking the experience and allowing us
to flow with it, he feels compelled to preach at us, lest we
explain the whole thing away with "some shallow physiological label."

This is an odd flaw in a writer whose enduring strength
is precisely the power to evoke. The stylistic split between
Blackwood the guru and Blackwood the ghost story writer
suggests that he is better off when he sticks to writing ghost
stories. Despite his protestations about being classified as
"the ghost man," his best scenes are his ghost scenes. It
scarcely matters whether we regard his apparitions as "psychic" or "homespun": they are as enchanting and chilling as
anything in the literature.

An unforgettable example is "The Willows," Blackwood's
most frequently anthologized tale. The elusive forces which
besiege the campers on a Danube island also besiege the
reader; they emerge as a deeply felt experience of "bewildering
beauty" and escalating terror. The story has its dull, jargon-
istic passages, but Blackwood mercifully keeps these to a
minimum. In the apparition scenes, Blackwood is a free-
wheeling pantheist: he envisions nature as an altogether
ambiguous divinity, impossible to pin down, both enticing
and insidious, spreading out into everything. The deadly
willow bushes, the strange sand-funnels, and the otherworldly
sounds which vibrate sometimes like gigantic gongs, sometimes like "the whirring of wings" and sometimes like "a
swarm of great invisible bees" are not lethal deities in themselves, but satellites of larger unknowable powers. Like sym-
bols in a Symbolist poem, they progressively suggest or evoke
each other without defining what they are moving toward.

In this important sense, Blackwood is part of the Le Fanu
tradition which opts for suggestion over definition. His best
stories ("Confession" and "The Haunted Island" are other

notable examples) are the ones which know how to keep a few
secrets: "The Willows" moves us precisely because we never
quite know what the Willows are. In classic Le Fanu fashion,
the story builds intensity through a slow accretion of detail:
the willow bushes which each day seem a little closer to the
tent; the otter-like creature "turning over and over in the
foaming waves" of the Danube; the "flying apparition"
which makes the sign of the cross as it glides by; the unexplainable destruction of the canoe; the "nude, fluid shapes"
which materialize in the patterns of the trees at night; the
multiplying sand funnels; the otherwordly gongs—all build
toward a conclusion that is at once climactic and mysterious.
Although interconnections between details gradually clarify
themselves, the larger structure of the "unearthly" region
remains a mystery.

This is not to say that Blackwood writes in the M. R. James
manner. The leisurely rise of intensity and the sudden falling
off at the end define the curve of the tale, but the intensity
at any given point is greater than in a James tale. James's
characteristic tension between form and substance, between
the story and the way the story is narrated, is foreign to
Blackwood, whose narrators are heavy-breathing converts to
occult theories. Lacking James's irony and sense of the particular, Blackwood attempts to infuse his language with an
intensity consistent with the "heightened consciousness" of
his narrators. His paucity of particularity and restraint is
consistent with his vision of a world where literally everything teems with hidden life.

Thus Blackwood's apparition scenes often contain multiple
apparitions of beings all the more ghostly for not being proper
ghosts:

> I saw it through a veil that hung before my eyes like the gauze
> drop-curtain used at the back of a theatre—hazily a little. It was
> neither a human figure nor an animal. To me it gave the strange
> impression of being as large as several animals grouped together, like
> horses, two or three, moving slowly. The Swede, too, got a similar
> result, though expressing it differently, for he thought it was shaped
> and sized like a clump of willow bushes, rounded at the top, and
> moving all over upon its surface—"coiling upon itself like smoke," he
> said afterwards. (45)

Focusing on the elusiveness of the apparition, Blackwood begins by telling us what it is not. Then, instead of one or two concrete Jamesian analogies, he hurls out chains of conditional similes. Most of these consist mysteriously of vehicles without tenors: "it" is like horses, like willows, and like smoke, but what is "it"? T. E. Lawrence once said that H. G. Wells's fantasy and science fiction stories give the illusion of being intensely visual without concretely visualizing anything.[15] Blackwood pulls the same seductive trick, giving us several metaphorical options with which to construct a subjective, tentative image. This strategy contrasts winningly with his discursive, doctrinal passages in which he tells us what to experience rather than allowing us to experience it.

As well as seeing the unseeable, Blackwood wants us to hear the unhearable. Some of the most majestic shudders in "The Willows" reach us through sound:

> We stood there, listening attentively together. At first I heard only the deep note of the water and the hissings rising from its turbulent surface. The willows, for once, were motionless and silent. Then a sound began to reach my ears faintly, a peculiar sound—something like the humming of a distant gong. It seemed to come across to us in the darkness from the waste of swamps and willows opposite. It was repeated at regular intervals, but it was certainly neither the sound of a bell nor the hooting of a distant steamer. I can liken it to nothing so much as to the sound of an immense gong, suspended far up in the sky, repeating incessantly its muffled metallic note, soft and musical, as it was repeatedly struck. My heart quickened as I listened.
> "I've heard it all day," said my companion. "While you slept this afternoon it came all round the island. I hunted it down, but could never get near enough to see—to localise it correctly. Sometimes it was overhead, and sometimes it seemed under the water. Once or twice, I could have sworn, it was not outside at all, but *within myself*—you know—the way a sound in the fourth dimension is supposed to come." (33)

This is Blackwood at his best and worst, illustrating his double role as creative artist and psychic instructor. It is disheartening to watch him derail his best metaphors with self-consciously didactic material. The impossibly clumsy reference to the fourth dimension at the end (especially given the disingenuous "you know") trivializes an otherwise magical scene. It is as if one of Blackwood's ears is as sensitive to exotic sounds as the ear of a Debussy, while the other ear is tone deaf. But the eerie splendor of the "immense gong" analogy makes Lovecraft's final judgment of Blackwood ("the one absolute and unquestioned master of weird atmosphere")[16] seem almost credible. It can be easily demonstrated that Blackwood often blunders by overwriting (that, as Barzun and Taylor put it, he "repeats his *Données* ").[17] He is obviously not as careful an artist as Hartley or M. R. James. On the other hand, he achieves grander effects when he succeeds.

Both the strengths and weaknesses in Blackwood are largely functions of his consuming interest in what Lovecraft calls "atmosphere." For Blackwood, "atmosphere" is fundamental and thematic rather than decorative. His dialogue and characterization often fall flat because he is more interested in recording intimations of the "beyond region" than in recording credible interactions between people.

Thematically, Blackwood's nature stories represent an early version of what D. H. Lawrence calls the "nonhuman." Indeed Blackwood has several things in common with Lawrence, the most noticeable of which is a repeated use of Lawrentian terms—"nonhuman," "otherness," "separateness," "the beyond"—before Lawrence codified them in *The Rainbow* and *Women in Love*.[18] Though not on the same level of achievement, Blackwood's rendering of nature is strikingly similar to Lawrence's in one crucial respect. Romantic poetry generally propounds the notion that interaction with nature enhances the individual's humanity. In the romantic universe, the emphasis is on the human. But Blackwood and Lawrence are part of a reactionary, anti-human thread which twists through writers such as Conrad, Yeats, Eliot, and Pound.[19] Rather than putting us in touch with our larger possibilities, communion with nature in Lawrence and Blackwood shows us that nature is a distinctly "other" form of life to which humanity is profoundly irrelevant. In "The Willows," nature is "another evolution not parallel to the human." While nature is not always this "alien" in Blackwood, it generally has the effect of making us aware of our smallness, our "utter insignificance" (8). Though not as apocalyptic as Lawrence, Blackwood is often as strident in his anti-human manifestoes:

"At any rate, here was a place unpolluted by men, kept clean by the winds from coarsening human influences" (38).

Blackwood's primitivism is Poe turned inside out. Instead of positing an "otherness," Poe creates settings which emerge from and embody the human psyche. The horror in Poe is the solipsistic horror of being entombed in one's own mind. Blackwood's fiction, like Lawrence's, represents a militant assertion that the outer world *does* exist—sublimely apart from human psychology. Although the unconscious is an active force in Blackwood's stories, it is not Freudian, not limited to human beings (or even "collective" human beings in a Jungian sense); it is a pre-human energy which infuses not only Lawrence's birds, beasts, and flowers, but patches of dirt.

This is somewhat of a departure from Le Fanu and Lovecraft, who present the alternate reality as an evil conspiracy. In Blackwood, the world beyond space and time is simply irrevocably *there*—not to be tampered with, but not evil either. Blackwood's distinctively "cosmic" fusion of horror and ecstasy occurs in this context: what the willows represent is alluring to people because it is superior; it is also deadly because it is saturated with a "primeval" intensity which "materialistic" modern man can no longer match.

Fortunately, Blackwood the Edwardian primitive is often belied by Blackwood the story-teller. His tendency to sentimentalize nature, even when nature does outrageous things, usually occurs in labored soliloquies by Blackwood personae (see "The South Wind")[20] or in passages of thinly disguised omniscient narration. "Blackwood's idea is that Nature is good, beautiful, right and healing," says Peter Penzoldt.[21] But it is difficult to reconcile this notion with "The Wendigo," a creature of the wind who snatches sleeping campers out of their tents at night, propels them for huge distances through the sky, and redeposits them on the ground as drooling idiots. This is peculiar behavior for something "beautiful, right and healing." The willows too, with their "sacrificial" habit of arbitrarily puncturing people to death with hideous pock marks, behave rather badly. If not evil, nature can at least be extraordinarily nasty. Ostensibly, human apparitions in old houses are evil (precisely because they are human), whereas "primeval" apparitions in nature are merely menacing. For the pursued character in the story, however, the distinction is likely to seem a dubious one.

Though more Gothic and "scary" in the usual sense, the indoor tales are similar in style and theme to the outdoor tales. In the better passages, they have the same hallucinatory vividness; in the weaker passages, the same lapses into pontification and repetitiveness. An example is "The Listener," an overlong but frequently powerful tale of a man haunted and possessed by the ghost of a suicidal leper.

"The Listener" has one very noticeable feature that the nature stories lack. In "The Willows," "The Wendigo," "Ancient Lights," "The Transfer," "The Glamour of the Snow", and "The Camp of the Dog," we experience Blackwood as an enormously sensual writer who seduces us into seeing, hearing, and smelling our way, into a transcendental experience. The tactile sense, however, is distinctly missing from these stories. Blackwood's "emissaries" of the wind, the trees, the snow, and the earth are too remote from modern, "mechanical" experience to be touchable or palpable. Blackwood was obviously in a different mood when he wrote "The Listener." In a marvelously jolting scene, the narrator accidentally touches something "cold and moist" in a dark room. "I felt the hair stir upon my head" (260)—and so do we, for the sense of touch has suddenly entered Blackwood's world. "The Listener" is relentlessly physical, conveying a constant sense of corrosive, rotting textures. Although the story is "cosmic" in its vision of an "invisible and malignant disease" in the universe, it is also a genuine horror tale in that it communicates that vision by exploiting all of the physical senses. As in Poe's "The Facts in the Case of M. Valdemar," each of the senses is given a distinct musical voice, gradually blending with the other voices in a dark fugue of sensations.

There is nothing cluttered or arbitrary about the intensity or density of language. The imagery organizes itself in discreet patterns which unconsciously prepare us for the climactic apparition scene. Most obvious are the smells: the entire story reeks of "strange, fetid" odors. More subtle are the colors, which finally coalesce into the appearance of the

Listener. The recurring grays, yellows, and greens spread into the story like the Listener's disease. When we witness a "dark, yellow-fog morning" early in the story or observe how "the fog poured up the dingy staircase in deep yellow coils," we know that the apparition is already in the process of materializing. In an uncanny sense, the entire story is "apparitional." Even the humor gives off a sickly residue of imagery. In a grotesquely amusing scene, the landlady serves the narrator two eggs, one of which is rotten. The narrator, understandably annoyed, demands that she replace the bad egg. The landlady, however, replaces the good egg with another bad one, "all green and yellow." When told that she has taken the wrong egg, she replies: "I thought the one I took down didn't smell so *very* bad" (249). The sensation of iciness is similarly related to the imagery of disease, connoting the clamminess of death and "frozen" powerlessness of the narrator: the stars shine "like points of ice in a blue-black sky"; the room is "as cold as a stone vault" (251). Also significant as both a premonition and actualization of the Listener is the consistent animal imagery: the narrator is haunted by an army of rats, by a "horde of immense cats," (261) and by the wind, which makes "a noise like the sudden sweeping of immense distant wings" (255). Finally, as the title suggests, the metaphor of listening is a constant, enveloping motif. The leprous presence hovers outside the narrator's door, listening, and the narrator listens to him listen. The sound of the Listener is again "not unlike the sound of wind" (260). The presence of natural elements is felt even in Blackwood's most claustrophobic houses.

This is Blackwood at his most compelling. The final apparition scene collects all of the previous imagery, creating a shuddery sense of culmination. Although we actually see the Listener for the first time, he has already appeared in subtle ways—on dark staircases, in dreams, and in the dense texture of the language:

> I woke suddenly, and saw a man in front of the dressing-table regarding himself in the mirror. The door was locked, as usual. I knew at once it was the Listener, and the blood turned to ice in my veins. Such a wave of horror and dread swept over me that it seemed to turn me rigid in the bed, and I could neither move nor speak. I noted, however, that the odour I so abhorred was strong in the room.

The man seemed to be tall and broad. He was stooping forward over the mirror. His back was turned to me, but in the glass I saw the reflection of a huge head and face illumined fitfully by the flicker of the night-light. The spectral grey of very early morning stealing in round the edge of the curtains lent an additional horror to the picture, for it fell upon hair that was tawny and mane-like, hanging loosely about a face whose swollen, rugose features bore the once seen never forgotten leonine expression of—I dare not write that awful word. But, by way of corroborative proof, I saw in the faint mingling of the two lights that there were several bronze-coloured blotches on the cheeks which the man was evidently examining with great care in the glass. The lips were pale and very thick and large. One hand I could not see, but the other rested on the ivory back of my hair-brush. Its muscles were strangely contracted, the fingers thin to emaciation, the back of the hand closely puckered up. It was like a big grey spider crouching to spring, or the claw of a great bird.

The full realization that I was alone in the room with this nameless creature, almost within arm's reach of him, overcame me to such a degree that, when he suddenly turned and regarded me with small beady eyes, wholly out of proportion to the grandeur of their massive setting, I sat bolt upright in bed, uttered a loud cry, and then fell back in a dead swoon upon the bed. (271-72)

One of the most fearful of all apparition scenes, the passage is a concentration of the motifs and visions which are laced throughout the story. Particularly effective is the way in which the constant yellowness of previous images intensifies into the "mane-like," "leonine" spectre of disease. Also remarkable are the multiple animal images. As he so often does, Blackwood gives us more than one poetic option: the hand of the Listener is "like a big grey spider crouching to spring, or the claw of a great bird." We view the scene as through an eerie kaleidoscope of interwoven visions. Most striking of all is the genuinely improvisational, "intuitive" quality of the writing, as if the imagistic patterns mysteriously interconnect of their own volition. This is the opposite of the feel of an M. R. James story, where we always sense precisely calculated effects.

The James approach has its distinct advantages, of course. As usual in Blackwood there is an awkward sentence which a more careful, less "spontaneous" artist would not have written. "I dare not write down that awful word" would never have gotten past James had he been Blackwood's editor. The sentence is of a piece with the "shock" ending, in which we hear the words that the narrator's friend "seemed almost afraid to utter: 'He was a leper!' " (275). The revelation is not nearly as shocking as Blackwood apparently thinks it is, especially since the reader has probably guessed it anyway. This is precisely the kind of melodramatic mannerism that the M. R. James school took such pains to exorcise from the modern ghostly tale.

"The Listener" is also useful as a structural paradigm of Blackwood's work. Frequently a character will begin by revolting against the every day world of empirical facts, with much fanfare about the visionary "path of real knowledge" and many regrets about having spent so much of life "in the pursuit of false knowledge, in the mere classifying and labelling of effects, the analysis of results."[22] The character then gradually propels himself into the experience of an alternate reality, only to find it necessary to flee back to the old "false" reality he has already declared to be an illusion of the senses. Worst of all, he usually finds that in order to make it back, he must enlist the aid of the "skeptical" character with whom he has been arguing throughout the story.

In "The Listener," the narrator spends a great deal of space sneering at his friend Chapter, the archetypal skeptic:

> He is a capital fellow, vigorous, healthy, with no nerves, and even less imagination. . . . Chapter always laughed at what he called my "fancies," being himself possessed only of that thin-blooded quality of imagination which is ever associated with the prosaic-minded man. Yet, if taunted with this obvious lack, his wrath is deeply stirred. His psychology is that of the crass materialist—always a rather funny article. It will afford me genuine relief, none the less, to hear the cold judgment his mind will have to pass upon the story of this house as I shall have it to tell. (269)

It is Chapter who, at the end of the story, arrives in time to save the narrator from the Listener: "The sight of his strong face and quiet eyes had an immediate effect upon me, and I grew calmer again. His very handshake was a sort of tonic. But, as I listened eagerly to the deep tones of his reassuring voice, and the visions of the night-time paled a little, I began to realise how very hard it was going to be to tell him my wild intangible tale. Some men radiate an animal vigour that destroys the delicate woof of a vision and effectually prevents its reconstruction. Chapter was one of those men" (273).

This is a typical Blackwood reversal in which the man of no imagination saves the visionary from his own visions. It is especially ironic that John Silence often collapses into the role of Chapter. In order to keep his patients from becoming "victims of higher space," he must "deaden their vibrations" and "block their entrances."[23] But the irony is lost on Blackwood, who seems only partially aware of the extreme ambivalence mirrored in his stories. Using the visionary character as his mouthpiece, he heaps pages of abuse on the "materialists" of the modern world, then drags them in at the end like cavalry to save the day. The stories announce themselves as allegories of the skeptic who learns his lesson, only to reverse themselves. It is the skeptics who survive—and enable the visionaries to survive as well. We are left with an ambivalence between vision and sanity that the stories never resolve.

The closest Blackwood comes to facing this ambivalence is, ironically, in one of his weakest, most bombastic stories, "May Day Eve." As usual, the character sees the dilemma and makes the decision by default. The difference is that this narrator makes the decision with an exact notion of the price he is paying: "I must escape at all costs and claim my old self again, however limited. I must have sanity, even if with limitations, but sanity at any price."[24] The "price" is a heavy one in Blackwood—a deadening of the imagination, the destruction of "the delicate woof of a vision." It is paradoxical that so many of the stories of this most mystical of ghost story writers should end on a ruthlessly pragmatic note. But since Blackwood's visions have a way of turning into horror stories, "sanity at any price" is not a bad bargain.

CHAPTER VI

CONCLUSION:
GHOST STORIES AS ENIGMAS

Beginning with Dorothy L. Sayers, anthology editors have repetitively introduced supernatural tales by trying to explain the impulse behind reading them. Most of their arguments—that supernatural horror is cathartic and therapeutic, that it implies the existence of good by showing us evil, that it provides a substitute for religion—are abstract and unconvincing. As we have seen, they are certainly belied by the stories themselves. Nevertheless, there is a curious tendency among editors to pretend that the tale of terror is not really terrible. The very least we can do is to insist that these stories mean business, that they are just what they purport to be.

Especially dubious is the notion, propounded chiefly by Christian apologists like Russell Kirk, that ghost stories preserve stable, "hierarchical" values in a skeptical age. What this literature actually does is move us toward an ever-darkening vision of chaos in a hostile universe. The supernatural exists, not as a force grounded in a coherent theology, but as an unaccountably destructive force which makes its own rules and chooses its own victims. If there is a teasing inconsistency here, the stories exploit rather than explain it; if the Devil is the principle of Chaos, he nevertheless seems to know what he is doing. In this vision, this strange Hardyesque blending of supernaturalism and skepticism, lies the power of these stories. The victim is often anonymous, almost never deserving the consequences that befall. The reader, identifying with the victim, realizes that he could as easily be pounced upon as

130

Mr. Jennings or Mr. Wraxall. It is difficult to imagine how we would be frightened by these stories if they provided neat revenge motives or comforting allegorical resolutions. The occasional providing of such comforts, usually in the weaker tales, only demonstrates that doom and horror are difficult for either writer or reader to swallow without a bromide every now and then. In their refusal to provide revenge motives, allegorical resolutions, or comforting moral platitudes, the better tales are surprisingly modern. Le Fanu is closer in his horror vision to Kafka and Conrad than to his contemporaries. M. R. James, Wakefield, Hartley, de la Mare, and the many others on our list are manifestly part of their age. Yet they often seem reluctant to be there. Unlike the surrealists, whom they sometimes resemble, they have a stake in wanting life to be orderly. In the works of Kafka, Vonnegut, Borges, and Marquez, existence is irrational from the outset—enough so for the magical to seem casual. The laws of nature and reason can cancel out on a moment's notice. In Kafka's "The Metamorphosis," a person turns into a cockroach in the first sentence, apparently because he feels like one. The careful realism of Kafka's prose occurs after, and continues to co-exist with, the shattering of reality, with no attempt to explain the contradiction. The ghost story does the reverse: it begins by assuming that life is rational and morally ordered, then begins to worry about that assumption when something inexplicably threatening creeps in.

With doubt comes a gradual dismemberment of the narrator's comfortably structured world. By the end of the story, some principle of darkness and disorder has made its presence felt. The survivors, if there are any, rarely know what to make of what almost did them in; but they do wonder about it, often grabbing for possible explanations from science, Christianity, Manichaeanism, animism, or any number of esoteric doctrines. Freudian readers of these stories have a more obvious and comforting explanation, but it is doubly unreliable since imposed from outside.

To surrender to the agnostic world of these stories is to admit, with the storyteller, that final explanations are beyond us. In the best stories—Le Fanu's "Green Tea" or Ramsey

Campbell's "The End of a Summer's Day"—it is this quality
of not knowing that makes us uneasy. Uncertainty is a reliable
conjurer of fear.

Even Blackwood, the most affirmative of ghost story
writers, envisions a world where values are unstable, life is
threatening, and human possibilities are blocked. The temporal, mortal world leads to ennui and oppression; but the
world of ghosts, the "beyond" realm of the imagination,
leads to madness and death. This dilemma explains why
Blackwood's endings are so problematic. His impulse to
affirm, to celebrate, does not lie comfortably within the boundaries of the form he has chosen to work within. Horror is as
much a part of his vision as affirmation, and he has a hard
time deciding which way to move at the end. Arthur Machen, a
similarly ambivalent writer, resolves the dilemma by simply
collapsing everything into horror at the end. It is perfectly
natural on the other hand, for Le Fanu or Wakefield, to write
grim endings: their endings are the inevitable, cumulative
working out of conspiracies set in motion by what Le Fanu
calls "the enormous machinery of hell." But Blackwood's
ambivalence results in stories which go in circles: his characters are "saved" by being thrown back into the bind that
caused them to get into trouble in the first place.

If horror and affirmation are difficult to integrate, horror
and humor are not. An ironic, ghoulish chuckle resounds
through this fiction, not as comic relief, but as an organic
element of supernatural horror. The deadpan sophistication
of Hartley and M. R. James, the farcical hyperbole of Blackwood, and the black humor of Le Fanu put us in touch with
one of the mysterious ironies of existence: that the most tran-
scendentally hideous experiences are frequently the funniest.
The tragi-comic situation in "Green Tea," that of an innocent
man literally harassed to death by an infernal monkey, is the
archetypal situation in this literature.

Yet for all its absurdity and ugliness, there is an undeniable
seductiveness about supernatural horror. At minimum, it provides an escape from the gritty, mundane horrors of everyday existence into the more exotic, subjective horrors of vision
and nightmare. The vampirized narrator of Le Fanu's "Car-

milla" speaks continually of horror as ecstasy, and her speeches echo through the works of Yeats, Machen, Onions, de la Mare, Lovecraft, and Blackwood. The more bookish M. R. James substitutes antiquarian nostalgia for overtly occultist experience as a means of flight from the dull present, with the same disastrous results.

That these stories do end disastrously for the characters suggests a theme which is always partially repressed, always on the verge of erupting. In these stories lies the tacit, half-buried admission that subjectivism, particularly of the occultist variety, is a self-destructive enterprise, a futile effort to escape the temporal and the human. The stories champion the off-beat, the fantastic, and the visionary, yet shrink from these experiences at the same time.

Examples of this split attitude are numerous. In Yeats's "Rosa Alchemica," Owen Aherne speaks of the desire for ghostly experience as a "thirst for destruction," a "search for an essence which would dissolve all mortal things."[1] Like Blackwood's visionaries, he travels well upwards into a "higher space," only to plummet desperately back down at the last instant. Seeking a "transmutation of the weary heart into the weariless spirit," he finds in the spirit world only a chaotic succession of "wild shapes rushing from despair to despair."[2] Michael Robartes, Aherne's more fanatically "unified" counterpart, never makes it back down. But Aherne always manages to slink back to the human world of "the weary spirit," of "mortality and tears," the world that his creator majestically celebrates in the late poems.

Another example of this self-recoiling vision is Oliver Onions' "The Beckoning Fair One, " a marvelously conceived story of a novelist who falls in love with his unfinished, ultimately murderous female creation. Onions, like Yeats, indentifies ghostly experience with the world of art, a world both ecstatic and demonic. The Beckoning Fair One represents the final triumph of the imagination, the subjective fusion of "joy" and "terror"; neither can be separated from the other, for both belong to the unified "category of absolute things."[3] When the narrator submits to The Beckoning Fair One, he also, unfortunately, submits to the loss of his sanity, becoming, as much as the expected other ghost, a deranged spectre who lowers all the blinds and haunts his own house (much as Brydon later does in Henry James's "The Jolly Corner").

Stories that involve an active seeking out of the uncanny almost always present this paradox: what is sought after— the otherworldly—makes us realize how much we need the worldly; but the more we know of the world, the more we need to be rid of it. The ideal is Blackwood's John Silence, a man who does some fancy stepping and manages to keep one foot in each world. But Dr. Silence is more of an abstract possibility (and an insufferable one at that) than a credible human being.

What unifies all of the better stories, whether of active seers or passive victims, is an unbroken sense of mystery and enigma. Nothing is more muddled and distorted than the common confusion of supernatural fiction with detective fiction and science fiction. Actually the latter two have far more in common with each other than either does with the ghost story. Science fiction and detective stories progress toward clarity, transparency, and explicit illumination of a puzzle or concept. They depend on the power of reason and logic; they invariably explain themselves. Ghost stories, however, sabotage the relationship between cause and effect. The parts are self-consistent, but they relate to an inexplicable, irrational whole. Instead of lighting up, the stories darken into shadowy ambiguity; instead of depending on logic, they depend on suggestion and connotation.

Stated another way, science fiction and detective stories concern themselves with content, with palpable ideas and events, whereas ghost stories concern themselves with language. We have seen repeatedly that the style delivers (or ruins) the shuddery experience far more than the plot. In the very best stories, such as de la Mare's "Seaton's Aunt" (the most ambiguous of all vampire stories) and Le Fanu's "The Child Who Went With the Fairies" (a fairy tale which diabolically transforms into a horror tale), the language is like the bite of the vampire or the "silver bell" voices of the fairies, draining and beguiling our better sense. Impossible to divorce from what happens in the story, the language is fundamental rather than decorative or "atmospheric." The suggestiveness of Le Fanu, the urbanity of M. R. James, and the effusiveness of Blackwood all ultimately conjure apparitions of words. These stories are ghostly poems which simply cannot be "told" around the stereotypical fire place. Someone must bring in a small lamp so that the teller can read them aloud.

As for the ultimate reasons why we read these stories, that tiresome, unanswerable question has already been raised too many times. That we enjoy them is enough. The reasons remain as perverse and mysterious as the stories themselves.

NOTES

INTRODUCTION

1. L. P. Hartley, "Introduction," *The Third Ghost Book*, ed. Cynthia Asquith (1955; rpt. New York, 1970), p. viii.

2. Richard Ellmann, *Eminent Domain* (1967; rpt. New York, 1970), p. 90.

3. See, for example, William Pfaff and Edmund Stillman, *The Politics of Hysteria* (1964; rpt. New York, 1965), pp. 111-115.

4. Samuel Hynes, *The Edwardian Turn of Mind* (1968; rpt. Princeton, 1971), p. 147.

5. Philip Van Doren Stern, "Introduction," *Great Ghost Stories* (1942; rpt. New York, 1947), pp. xvi-xvii.

6. T. S. Eliot, "Introduction," Charles Williams, *All Hallows Eve* (1948; rpt. New York, 1967), p. xv.

7. Russell Kirk, *The Surly Sullen Bell* (New York, 1962), pp. 238-39.

8. Edmund Wilson, *Classics and Commercials* (New York, 1962), p. 173.

9. H. P. Lovecraft, *Supernatural Horror in Fiction* (1927; rpt. New York, 1973), p. 82.

10. *Ibid.*, p. viii.

11. *Ibid.*, p. 102.

12. Tzvetan Todorov's related structuralist study, *The Fantastic* (New York, 1970), is an analysis not of the supernatural, but of the "apparently supernatural" in fiction. "The fantastic" is a genre based on "hesitation." Once a story moves into the world of the supernatural, it must be assigned to our genre, "the marvelous."

13. Virginia Woolf, "Henry James's Ghosts," in *The Turn of the Screw: Essays in Criticism*, ed. Robert Kimbrough (New York, 1966), p. 179.

14. See Edel's commentary in *Ghostly Tales of Henry James* (New York, 1949) and Henry James, *Stories of the Supernatural* (New York, 1970).

15. Peter Penzoldt, *The Supernatural in Fiction* (London, 1952), pp. 254-55.

16. Hartley, p. vii.

17. Hynes, p. 147.

18. Stern, p. xvi.

19. Wilson, p. 288.

20. Lovecraft, p. 16.

21. *Best Ghost Stories of J. S. Le Fanu*, ed. E. F. Bleiler (New York, 1964), p. 444.

22. Basil Davenport, "On Telling Stories," *Tales to Be Told in the Dark* (New York, 1953), p. vii.

23. Robert Aickman, "Introduction," *The Fontana Book of Great Ghost Stories* (New York, 1966), pp. 7-8.

24. Dorothy L. Sayers, "Introduction," *The Third Omnibus of Crime* (New York, 1942), p.5.

CHAPTER I

1. Oliver Onions "Credo," *The Collected Ghost Stories of Oliver Onions* (New York, 1971), p. X.

2. V. S. Pritchett, *The Living Novel and later Appreciations* (New York, 1947), pp. 121-28; Edna Kenton, "A Forgotten Creator of Ghosts," *The Bookman*, 1929, pp. 528-35; *Minor Classics of Nineteenth Century Fiction*, Vol. II, ed. William E.

Buckler (Boston, 1967), pp. 27-28; Nelson Browne, *Sheridan Le Fanu* (New York, 1951), pp. 78-80; E. F. Benson, "Sheridan Le Fanu," *The Spectator*, 21 Feb. 1931, p. 264.

3.   M. R. James, "Introduction," *Ghosts and Marvels* (London, 1927), p. vi.

4.   *Best Ghost Stories of J. S. Le Fanu*, ed. E. F. Bleiler (New York, 1964), p. 182. Unless otherwise noted, further quotations from Le Fanu's tales will be documented by citing page numbers from the Bleiler edition.

5.   On the rare occasions when Le Fanu directly quotes a demon's speech, he is careful to include diabolical transformation as a key element in the story. Thus Carmilla speaks, but only in her nonvampiric phases.

6.   Penzoldt, p. 77; Pritchett, pp. 122-23; Michael H. Begnal, *Joseph Sheridan Le Fanu* (Lewisburg, Pa., 1971), p. 40; James, p. vi.

7.   S. M. Ellis, *Wilkie Collins, Le Fanu and Others* (London, 1931), p. 165. "Tragic" is more applicable to the novels than to the tales. (Ellis finds "a sort of stately inevitableness" in *The House by the Churchyard*.)

8.   The most extreme psychoanalytical view of the tale is John S. Hill, "The Dual Hallucination in 'The Fall of the House of Usher,' " *Southwest Review*, XLVIII (1963), 396-402.

9.   Neither Ellis nor Browne does any more than mention the connection.

10.   Edgar Allan Poe, "The Pit and the Pendulum," *The Complete Tales and Poems of Edgar Allan Poe* (New York, 1938), p. 246.

11.   Herman Melville, "Hawthorne and His Mosses," reprinted in "Reviews and Letters by Melville," *Moby Dick*, ed. Harrison Hayford and Hershel Parker (New York, 1967), p. 540.

12.   With the exception of "Green Tea," none of these confrontations are ever dramatized. Though frequently mentioned in prologues, Hesselius never appears as a character in any of the other tales. Even in "Green Tea," the therapy is interrupted by the patient's suicide before we are able to assess its effectiveness. Unlike Machen's Dr. Raymond, Blackwood's John Silence or Hodgson's Dr. Carnacki (all of whom he anticipates), Hesselius is a background rather than a luminary figure.

13.   Of all the writers who attempted this fusion—Stevenson, Bulwer-Lytton, Machen, Blackwood, Hodgson, and Wells (among others)—only Wells seems to have recognized that the polarities must be reconciled with the aesthetic demands of the story as well as with each other. Compare Wells's "The Plattner Story" with Bulwer-Lytton's "The House and the Brain": one is an integrated work of fiction, the other a story interrupted (and subverted) by an essay.

14.   Buckler, p. 27.

15.   Although brief, "The Moonlit Road" achieves an almost mind-numbing complexity by emerging from three fragmented points of view, including that of the murder victim as communicated through a medium. "The Suitable Surroundings" juxtaposes time sequences as well as narrators, in each case creating a maximum of confusion which gives the tale a peculiarly delayed impact.

16.   Benson, pp. 263-64.

CHAPTER II

1.   Dorothy Scarborough, *The Supernatural in Modern English Fiction* (1917; rpt. New York, 1967).

2.   Lovecraft, p. 43. In his introduction to the Dover edition, E. F. Bleiler speculates that Lovecraft knew Le Fanu only by name.

3.   *The Cambridge History of English Literature*, ed. Sir A. W. Ward and A. R. Waller, XIV (New York, 1917).

4. James Payn, *Some Literary Recollections* (New York, 1884), pp. 183-84.

5. *The Short Stories of Henry James*, ed. Clifton Fadiman (New York, 1945), p. 126.

6. James was probably referring to *Uncle Silas*, Le Fanu's most popular and easily most enduring novel. The most penetrating commentary on the novels is found in Elizabeth Bowen's introduction to *The House by the Churchyard* (London, 1968). Bowen points out that Le Fanu's treatment of the supernatural in his longer fiction is "matter-of-fact though nonetheless terrifying." She also admires "his depiction of servants, together with more irregular hirelings. . . . The intimacy, the complicity, the often-shared desperations of the employer-employed relationship, as it is in Ireland, can seldom have been, and may never be, better drawn." The novels thus look outward to Irish society in a way that the tales do not attempt.

7. M. R. James, "Prologue," Joseph Sheridan Le Fanu, *Madam Crowl's Ghost and Other Tales of Mystery* (London, 1923).

8. H. R. Wakefield, "Farewell to All Those," *Strayers From Sheol* (Sauk City, Wis., 1961), p. 4. A. C. and E. F. Benson were among the group of friends to whom James would read his tales aloud.

9. James, "Introduction," *Ghosts and Marvels*, p. vi.

10. Browne, pp. 16-17.

11. Typical examples are August Derleth's "An Introduction to H. P. Lovecraft" in *The Haunter of the Dark and Other Tales* (London, 1963), and Philip Van Doren Stern's introduction to Machen's *Tales of Horror and the Supernatural* (New York, 1948).

12. Bleiler, p. 10.

13. This was the impossibly rare *Ghost Stories and Tales of Mystery* (London, 1851), of which only four copies are known to exist. For bibliographical information on this and other rare Le Fanu volumes, see S. M. Ellis, *Wilkie Collins, Le Fanu and Others* (London, 1931).

14. Ellis, p. 175.

15. *Ibid.*, p. 177.

16. The closest contender is Ambrose Bierce who, like one of his own characters in "Mysterious Disappearances," managed to mysteriously disappear.

17. An exception is "The Familiar," which is every bit as controlled as the other Hesselius tales, but was written more than twenty years earlier. Le Fanu simply added the Hesselius material before reprinting the story in *In A Glass Darkly*. The history of "The Familiar" illustrates the difficulty of generalizing about early versus late Le Fanu.

18. For examples, see "The Dead Sexton" and "Sir Dominick's Bargain," both reprinted in Bleiler.

19. Old Sally is a character in *The House By the Churchyard*. Montague Summers was the first to anthologize the episode as a separate tale, cleverly presenting it as "An Authentic Narrative of the Ghost of a Hand."

20. The ghost bears a more than passing resemblance to Chief Justice Harbottle, especially given the rarity of fat ghosts in Le Fanu and the author's use of Harbottle as a symbol of motiveless evil in two other tales.

21. The tale was reprinted in two supernatural formats: *The Purcell Papers* (1880) and *A Chronicle of Golden Friars and Other Stories* (1896).

22. The *Dublin University Magazine*, June, 1838, p. 728.

23. *Ibid.*, p. 729.

24. J. S. Le Fanu, *Ghost Stories and Mysteries*, ed. E. F. Bleiler (New York, 1975), p. 333.

25. *Ibid.*, p. 372.

26. *Ibid.*, p. 369.

27. *Ibid.*, p. 371.

28. *Ibid.*, p. 125. This is the second of the *Ghost Stories of Chapelizod*; it is by far the most horrific tale in the series.

29. As a contemporary exponent of the English horror tradition, Campbell is an important figure. He is probably the best living writer of supernatural horror fiction.

30. *Ibid.*, p. 182.

31. *Ibid.*

32. Examples of works which share the same concept include "The Fortunes of Sir Robert Ardagh," "Sir Dominick's Bargain" and *The Haunted Baronet*; "Passage in the Secret History of an Irish Countess," "The Murdered Cousin" and *Uncle Silas*; "A Chapter in the History of a Tyrone Family" and *The Wyvern Mystery*; and "Some Account of the Latter Days of the Hon. Richard Marston of Dunoran" and "The Evil Guest." Le Fanu was obviously fond of expanding themes from his short stories into novels.

33. The tone of the Society's published *Proceedings* was scrupulously, self-consciously scientific, even when the content had to do with such things as the Haunted Houses Committee report. In addition, however, there is a quality of hesitation and nervous qualification in many of these reports which contrasts sharply with Hesselius's sweeping proclamations and generalities. For detailed examples and analyses of the Society's publications, see Samuel Hynes, *The Edwardian Turn of Mind* and the "Notes and Sources" from the Norton Critical Edition of James's *Turn of the Screw*, ed. Robert Kimbrough (New York, 1966).

34. For examples, see Edward Wagenknecht, "Introduction," Walter de la Mare, *Eight Tales* (Sauk City, Wis., 1971), p. xix; Quentin Anderson, "Introduction," Nathaniel Hawthorne, *Twice-Told Tales and Other Short Stories* (New York, 1960), p. xi; and H. P. Lovecraft on M. R. James in *Supernatural Horror in Literature*, p. 101.

35. Edel, "Introduction," *Ghostly Tales of Henry James*, p. viii.

36. Ellis's account of "The Familiar" is characteristic: "It is a crescendo of horror. At first he (Barton) is conscious of footsteps dogging him at lonely spots. They intensify. In time, the malignant Watcher becomes visible. Then the appalling death scene, where the author skillfully leaves to the imagination what supreme terror finally wrested poor Barton's shuddering soul from his body" (Ellis, p. 156).

37. Ellis, p. 156.

38. For an extensive bibliography of works on vampire mythology, see Leonard Wolf, *A Dream of Dracula* (New York, 1972), pp. 321-26.

39. Laura's assertion that no vampires have appeared since Carmilla (336) is inconclusive. According to Vordenburg, victims develop into vampires while "in the grave" and rise again after an unknown passage of time.

40. Browne, p. 84.

41. See especially "A Chapter In the History of A Tyrone Family" (1839), the gruesome prototype of *Jane Eyre*.

42. Samuel Beckett, *Watt* (1953; rpt. New York, 1959), pp. 201-02.

43. Benson, 264.

44. E. F. Bleiler, "Introduction," *The Collected Ghost Stories of Mrs. J. H. Riddell* (New York, 1977), p. xvii.

CHAPTER III

1. M. R. James, *Collected Ghost Stories* (1931; rpt. New York, 1974), pp. 112-113.

Further quotations from James's stories will be documented by citing page numbers from the text.

2.   Even H. P. Lovecraft comments on the appropriateness of these techniques, despite his failure to use them in his own fiction. See Lovecraft, *Supernatural Horror in Fiction.*

3.   S. G. Lubbock, *A Memoir of Montague Rhodes James* (Cambridge, 1939), p. 37.

4.   *Ibid.*

5.   *Madam Crowl's Ghost and Other Tales of Mystery* (1923).

6.   Peter Fleming, "The Stuff of Nightmares." *Spectator Literary Supplement,* 18 April 1931, p. 633.

7.   The new, handsome St. Martin's Press edition of James's collected stories was reviewed enthusiastically in the 7 July 1975 edition of the *Village Voice.*

8.   Stephen Gaselee, *Proceedings of the British Academy,* 1936, XXII, 424.

9.   *Ibid.*

10.   James, "Prologue," Sheridan Le Fanu, *Madam Crowl's Ghost,* p. vii.

11.   Gaselee, p. 430.

12.   Lubbock, p. 39.

13.   James, p. vii.

14.   *Ibid.*

15.   *Ibid.,* p. 9.

16.   James, "Introduction," *Ghosts and Marvels,* p. vi.

17.   L. P. Hartley, Ramsey Campbell, and Walter de la Mare are similar to James in this respect. But many writers in the genre—including Arthur Machen, H. P. Lovecraft, and Algernon Blackwood—feel a tiresome obligation to treat hackneyed situations and tropes as if the reader had never encountered them before.

18.   From an interview with James included in a review of *Madam Crowl's Ghost* published in the Morning Post, 9 October 1923, p. 11.

19.   *Ibid.*

20.   James, *Madam Crowl's Ghost,* p. vii.

21.   *Ibid.*

22.   See Malden's "The Thirteenth Tree" in *Nine Ghosts* (London, 1943). See also Swain's "The Man with the Roller" in *Stoneground Ghost Tales* (Cambridge, 1912). Stylistically as well as conceptually, Swain and Malden are closer to James than to any other writers in the field.

23.   For a further development of this motif, see the stories in L. T. C. Rolt's superb *Sleep No More* (London, 1948). An engineer by profession, Rolt is a master of situations involving haunted mines, canals and various kinds of machinery. Especially effective is "Hawley Bank Foundry," a tale which demonstrates that terror can emerge from the most unlikely settings.

24.   Quoted by Russell Kirk in the epilogue to his collection of ghost stories, *The Surly Sullen Bell* (New York, 1964), p. 157.

25.   M. R. James, "Preface," *Ghost Stories of an Antiquary* (1904; rpt. New York, 1971), p. 8.

26.   Though interest in James appears to be growing (see note 7), it is still nowhere near as large as interest in the Lovecraft circle or in contemporary writers such as William Blatty, Thomas Tryon, and Stephen King.

27.   Malden, p. 5.

28.   Alfred Hitchcock, "Preface," *Fourteen of My Favorites in Suspense,* ed. Alfred Hitchcock (New York, 1959), p. 9.

CHAPTER IV

1. Lovecraft, *Supernatural Horror in Fiction*, p. 101.

2. Edward Wagenknecht, "Introduction," Walter de la Mare, *Eight Tales* (Sauk City, Wis., 1971), p. xiii.

3. *Ibid.*, pp. 96-97.

4. *Ibid.*, p. 108.

5. *Ibid.*, p. 104.

6. *Ibid.*, p. 106.

7. E. F. Benson, *The Room in the Tower* (London, 1912), p. 206.

8. Jaques Barzun and Wendell H. Taylor, *A Catalogue of Crime* (New York, 1971; Second Impression Corrected, 1974), p. 720.

9. Quoted in *Books From Arkham House*, ed. Roderic Meng (Sauk City, Wis., 1972), p. 18.

10. H. R. Wakefield, "Why I Write Ghost Stories," *The Clock Strikes Twelve* (New York, 1946), p. 7.

11. H. R. Wakefield, "Introduction," *Strayers from Sheol* (Sauk City, Wis., 1961), p. 3.

12. *Ibid.*, pp. 3-4.

13. Wakefield, *The Clock Strikes Twelve*, p. 34.

14. H. R. Wakefield, *Others Who Returned* (New York, 1929), p. 23.

15. *Ibid.*, p. 34.

16. *The Third Omnibus of Crime*, Dorothy Sayers, ed., p. 780.

17. Wakefield, *Strayers from Sheol*, p. 136.

18. Barzun and Taylor, p. 720.

19. Paul Bloomfield, *L. P. Hartley* (London, 1962), p. 1.

20. *Ibid.*

21. Hartley, "Introduction," *The Third Ghost Book*, p. vii.

22. Quoted by Peter Bien in *L. P. Hartley* (London, 1963), p. 246.

23. *Ibid.*, p. 11.

24. Hartley, "Introduction," p. vii.

25. L. P. Hartley, *The Travelling Grave* (Sauk City, Wis., 1948), p. 196.

26. *Ibid.*, p. 127.

27. *Ibid.*, p. 232.

28. See Freud's "The Uncanny" in Sigmund Freud, *On Creativity and the Unconscious*, ed. Benjamin Nelson (New York, 1958).

29. Hartley, *The Travelling Grave*, pp. 9-11.

30. *Ibid.*, p. 20.

31. *Ibid.*, p. 197.

32. *Ibid.*, p. 48.

33. Bien, pp. 100-101.

34. Hartley, *The Travelling Grave*, p. 84.

35. Aickman, "Introduction," *The Fontana Book of Great Ghost Stories*.

36. Hartley, *The Travelling Grave*, pp. 52-54.

37. Aickman, p. 8.

38. R. H. Malden, "Preface," *Nine Ghosts* (London, 1943), p. 5.

39. E. G. Swain, "Dedication" in *Stoneground Ghost Tales* (Cambridge, 1912).

40. James, "Preface," *Ghost Stories of an Antiquary*, p. 8.

41. Malden, p. 110.

42. *Ibid.*, p. 66.
43. Swain, p. 23.
44. *Ibid.*, p. 101.
45. *Ibid.*, pp. 23-24.

CHAPTER V

1. *Best Ghost Stories of Algernon Blackwood*, ed. E. F. Bleiler (New York, 1973), p. 230. Unless otherwise indicated, further quotations from Blackwood's stories will be documented by citing page numbers from the Bleiler edition.

2. See especially Penzoldt's chapter on Blackwood.

3. Arthur Machen, *Tales of Horror and the Supernatural* (1949; rpt. New York, 1971), p. 107.

4. See Felix Morrow, "Introduction," *The Best Supernatural Tales of Algernon Blackwood* (New York, 1973), pps. v-x. An advocate of what *Ramparts* calls the "New Mysticism," Morrow views Blackwood as a precursor of the Cosmic Consciousness of the 1970's. According to Morrow, Blackwood shows us "the hope and glory in the illimitable possibilities of human consciousness . . . his imagination provides us the knowledge which the race has not yet mastered."

5. Algernon Blackwood, *The Empty House* (1906; rpt. London, 1964), p. 154.

6. *Ibid.*, p. 172.

7. Derek Hudson, "A Study of Algernon Blackwood," *Essays and Studies* (London, 1961), p. 104.

8. Bleiler, "Introduction," *Best Ghost Stories of Algernon Blackwood*, p. x.

9. Rudson, p. 102.

10. Algernon Blackwood, *Tales of Terror and the Unknown* (1964; rpt. New York, 1965), p. 329.

11. Hudson, p. 113.

12. Blackwood, "Author's Preface," *Tales of Terror and the Unknown*, p. 8.

13. Lovecraft, *Supernatural Horror in Literature*, p. 96.

14. Blackwood, *Tales of Terror and the Unknown*, p. 177.

15. T. E. Lawrence, review of H. G. Wells's *Collected Stories*, *The Spectator*, 28 Feb., 1928, pp. 268-9.

16. Lovecraft, p. 95.

17. Barzun and Taylor, p. 701.

18. See especially chapters I and II of *The Rainbow* and chapter XI of *Women in Love*.

19. For a thorough study of the politics of the modern masters, see John R. Harrison, *The Reactionaries* (New York, 1966).

20. Algernon Blackwood, *Pan's Garden* (London, 1912), p. 105.

21. Penzoldt, p. 236.

22. Blackwood, *Tales of Terror and the Unknown*, p. 190.

23. Algernon Blackwood, *Tales of the Mysterious and Macabre* (London, 1967), p. 397.

24. Blackwood, *Tales of Terror and the Unknown*, p. 189.

CHAPTER VI

1. William Butler Yeats, *Mythologies* (1959; rpt. New York, 1969), p. 270.

2. *Ibid.*, p. 269.

3. *The Collected Ghost Stories of Oliver Onions* (New York, 1971), p. 38.

A SELECTED BIBLIOGRAPHY
OF GHOSTLY FICTION

(Note: To make the reader's search easier,
I have emphasized recent over rare editions.)

Aickman, Robert. *Cold Hand in Mine: Strange Stories.* New York: Scribner's, 1977.

————, ed. *The Fontana Book of Great Ghost Stories.* New York: Beagle, 1966.

Asquith, Cynthia, ed. *The Ghost Book.* 3 vols. 1927, 1952; rpt. New York: Beagle, 1970-71.

————, ed. *Shudders.* New York: Scribner's, 1929.

————. *This Mortal Coil.* Sauk City, Wis.: Arkham House, 1947.

Benson, A. C. *The Hill of Trouble and Other Stories.* London: Ibister, 1903.

————. *Paul, the Minstrel and Other Stories.* New York: Putnam, 1912.

Benson, E. F. *More Spook Stories.* London: Hutchinson, 1934.

————. *The Room in the Tower.* London: Mills and Boon, 1912.

————. *Spook Stories.* London: Hutchinson, 1928.

————. *Visible and Invisible.* New York: Doran, 1923.

Benson, R. H. *The Light Invisible.* London: Ibister, 1903.

————. *The Mirror of Shallot.* London: Benziger Brothers, 1907.

Bierce, Ambrose. *Can Such Things Be?* Washington: Neale, 1903.

————. *Collected Writings.* New York: Citadel, 1946.

————. *Ghost and Horror Stories of Ambrose Bierce.* Ed. E. F. Bleiler. New York: Dover, 1964.

Blackwood, Algernon. *Ancient Sorceries and Other Stories.* Harmondsworth, Middlesex, England: Penguin, 1968.

————. *Best Ghost Stories of Algernon Blackwood.* Ed. E. F. Bleiler. New York: Dover, 1973.

————. *The Best Supernatural Tales of Algernon Blackwood.* New York: Causeway, 1973.

————. *The Dance of Death and Other Tales.* New York: Dial Press, 1928.

————. *The Doll and One Other.* Sauk City, Wis.: Arkham House, 1946.

————. *Day and Night Stories.* New York: Dutton, 1917.

————. *The Empty House.* 1906; rpt. London: John Baker, 1964.

————. *Incredible Adventures.* New York: Macmillan, 1914.

————. *John Silence, Physician Extraordinary.* 1908; London, John Baker, 1969.

————. *The Listener and Other Stories.* 1907; rpt. London, Eveleigh Nash, 1930.

————. *The Lost Valley and Other Stories.* London: Eveleigh Nash, 1910.

————. *Pan's Garden.* London: MacMillan, 1912.

————. *Shocks.* New York: Dutton, 1936.

————. *Tales of the Mysterious and Macabre.* 2 vols. London: Spring, 1967.

————. *Tales of Terror and the Unknown.* 1964; rpt. New York: Dutton, 1965.

————. *Ten Minute Stories.* London: John Murray, 1914.

————. *Tongues of Fire and Other Sketches.* London: Jenkins, 1924.

Bowen, Elizabeth. *The Cat Jumps.* London: Jonathan Cape, 1934.

Bowen, Marjorie. *Kecksies and Other Twilight Tales.* Sauk City, Wis.: Arkham House, 1973.

————. *The Last Bouquet. Some Twilight Tales.* London: J. Lane, 1933.

Bulwer-Lytton, Lord Edward G. *The Haunted and the Haunters; or The House and the Brain. Minor Classics of Nineteenth Century Fiction.* Ed. William E. Buckler. 2 vols. Boston: Riverside, 1967.

Campbell, Ramsey. *Demons by Daylight.* Sauk City, Wis.: Arkham House, 1973.

————. *The Height of the Scream.* Sauk City, Wis.: Arkham House, 1967.

————, ed. *Superhorror.* New York: St. Martin's, 1977.

Cerf, Bennett, ed., *Famous Ghost Stories.* New York: Random House, 1944.

Chambers, R. W. *The King in Yellow.* Ed. E. F. Bleiler. New York: Dover, 1970.

Collier, John. *The John Collier Reader.* New York: Knopf, 1972.

Collins, Wilkie. *Tales of Terror and the Supernatural.* New York: Dover, 1972.

Conrad, Joseph. *Heart of Darkness.* 1902; rpt. New York: Norton Critical, 1971.

————. "The Idiots." *Tales of Unrest.* New York: Doubleday, 1928.

Crawford, F. Marion. *Wandering Ghosts.* London: Unwin, 1911.

Coppard, A. E. *The Collected Tales of A. E. Coppard.* New York: Knopf, 1951.

Dahl, Roald. *Kiss Kiss.* 1953; rpt. New York: Dell, 1961.

————. *Someone Like You.* 1948; rpt. New York: Dell, 1961.

Davenport, Basil, ed. *Tales to be Told in the Dark.* New York: Dodd, Meade, 1953.

De la Mare, Walter. *The Connoisseur and Other Stories.* New York: Knopf, 1926.

————. *Eight Tales.* Sauk City, Wis.: Arkham House, 1971.

————. *On the Edge.* London: Faber, 1930.

————. *The Riddle and Other Tales.* New York: Knopf, 1930.

Doyle, Arthur Conan. *Tales of Terror and Mystery.* New York: Doubleday, 1977.

Fraser, Phyllis and Wise, Herbert. *Great Tales of Terror and the Supernatural.* New York: Modern Library, 1944.

Gray, Arthur. *Tedious Brief Tales of Granta and Gramarye.* London: W. Heffer and Sons, 1919.

Haining, Peter, ed. *The Unspeakable People.* New York: Popular Library, 1969.

Hardy, Thomas. *Wessex Tales.* New York: Harper and Brothers, 1896.

Hartley, L. P. *The Killing Bottle.* London and New York: Putnam, 1932.

————. *Night Fears.* London: Putnam, 1924.

————. *The Travelling Grave and Other Stories.* Sauk City, Wis., Arkham House, 1948.

Harvey, W. F. *The Beast with Five Fingers and Other Tales.* 1928; rpt. New York: Dutton, 1947.

————. *Midnight House and Other Tales.* London: Dent, 1910.

————. *Midnight Tales.* London: Dent, 1946.

Hawthorne, Nathaniel. *Hawthorne's Short Stories.* New York: Vintage, 1946.

————. *Twice-Told Tales.* 1837; rpt. New York: Washington Square Press, 1960.

Heard, H. F. *The Great Fog and Other Weird Tales.* New York: Vanguard, 1944.

Hearn, Lafcadio. *Kwaidan: Stories and Studies of Strange Things.* 1904; rpt. New York: Dover, 1968.

————. *Some Chinese Ghosts.* 1887; rpt. New York: Modern Library, 1927.

Hitchcock, Alfred, ed. *Bar the Doors.* New York: Dell, 1946.

Hodgson, William Hope. *Carnacki the Ghost Finder.* 1913; rpt. London: Panther, 1973.

————. *Deep Waters.* 1914; rpt. Sauk City, Wis.: Arkham House, 1967.

————. *The Luck of the Strong.* London: Eveleigh Nash, 1916.

————. "The Voice in the Night." *The Fontana Book of Great Ghost Stories.* Ed. Robert Aickman. New York: Beagle, 1966.

Jackson, Shirley. *The Lottery.* New York: Avon, 1969.

Jackson, T. G. *Six Ghost Stories.* London: John Murray, 1919.

James, Henry. *Ghostly Tales of Henry James.* Ed. Leon Edel. New York: Grosset and Dunlap, 1949.

————. *Stories of the Supernatural.* Ed. Leon Edel. New York: Taplinger, 1970.

James, M. R. *The Collected Ghost Stories of M. R. James.* London: Arnold, 1931. St. Martin's edition, 1974.

————. *Ghost Stories of an Antiquary.* Ed. E. F. Bleiler. 1904; rpt. New York: Dover, 1971. (See also the 1974 Penguin edition, which contains *More Ghost Stories of an Antiquary* in the same edition.)

Kersh, Gerald. *Men Without Bones.* New York: Paperback Library, 1962.

————. *Nightshades and Damnations.* New York: Fawcett, 1968.

Kipling, Rudyard. *Phantoms and Fantasies.* New York: Doubleday, 1965.

————. *The Phantom Rickshaw and Other Stories.* 1898; rpt. New York: Standard Classics, 1930.

————. *Selected Prose and Poetry.* Garden City, New York: Garden City, 1937.

Kirk, Russell. *The Surly Sullen Bell.* New York: Fleet, 1962.

Klein, T. E. D. "The Events at Poroth Farm." *The Year's Best Horror Stories.* Vol. II. Ed. Richard Davis. New York: Daw, 1972.

Lamb, Hugh, ed. *A Wave of Fear.* New York: Taplinger, 1973.

————, ed. *Return from the Grave.* New York: Taplinger, 1976.

Lee, Vernon. *For Maurice; Five Unlikely Stories.* London: J. Lane, 1927.

————. *Hauntings: Fantastic Stories.* London: J. Lane, 1906.

————. *Pope Jacynth and Other Fantastic Tales.* London: J. Lane, 1907.

————. *The Snake Lady and Other Stories.* New York: Grove Press, 1954.

LeFanu, J. S. *Best Ghost Stories.* Ed. E. F. Bleiler. New York: Dover, 1964.

————. "The Last Heir of Castle Connor." *Dublin University Magazine,* June 1838, pp. 728-29.

————. *Ghost Stories and Mysteries.* Ed. E. F. Bleiler. New York: Dover, 1975.

————. *The Hours after Midnight.* Ed. Des Hickey. London: Leslie Frewin, 1975.

————. *The Purcell Papers.* Ed. August Derleth. 1880; rpt. Sauk City, Wis.: Arkham House, 1975.

Lovecraft, H. P. *At the Mountains of Madness.* Ed. August Derleth. Sauk City, Wis.: Arkham House, 1964.

————. *Dagon and Other Macabre Tales.* Ed. August Derleth. Sauk City, Wis.: Arkham House, 1965.

————. *The Dunwich Horror.* Ed. August Derleth. Sauk City, Wis.: Arkham House, 1963.

————. *The Haunter of the Dark.* London: Panther, 1963.

————. *The Horror in the Museum and Other Revisions.* Ed. August Derleth. Sauk City, Wis.: Arkham House, 1970.

Machen, Arthur. *Tales of Horror and the Supernatural.* 2 vols. 1949; rpt. New York: Pinnacle, 1971.

Malden, R. H. *Nine Ghosts.* London: Arnold, 1943.

McCauley, Kirby, ed. *Night Chills.* New York, Avon, 1975.

————, ed. *Frights*. New York: St. Martin's Press, 1976.

Munby, A. N. L. *The Alabaster Hand*. London: Dobson, 1942.

Onions, Oliver. *Collected Ghost Stories*. New York: Dover, 1971.

Poe, Edgar Allan. *Complete Tales and Poems*. New York: Random House, 1938.

Quiller-Couch, Arthur. *I Saw Three Ships and Other Winter's Tales*. London: Cassell, 1892.

————. *Old Fires and Profitable Ghosts*. New York: Scribner's, 1900.

————. *Two Sides of the Face: Midnight Tales*. New York: Scribner's: 1903.

————. *Wandering Heath: Stories, Studies and Sketches*. New York: Scribner's, 1895.

————. *The White Wolf and Other Fireside Tales*. New York: Scribner's, 1902.

Riddell, Mrs. J. H. *The Collected Ghost Stories*. Ed. E. F. Bleiler. New York: Dover, 1977.

Rolt, L. T. C. *Sleep No More*. London, Constable, 1948.

Sayers, Dorothy L., ed. *The Omnibus of Crime*. Vol. I. New York: Harcourt, Brace, 1929.

————, ed. *The Second Omnibus of Crime*. New York: Blue Ribbon, 1932.

————, ed. *The Third Omnibus of Crime*. New York: Coward McCann, 1942.

Scott, Eleanor. *Randall's Round*. London: Ernest Benn. 1929.

Scott, Sir Walter. "The Tapestried Chamber." *Walk in Dread*. Ed. Dorothy Tomlinson. New York: Taplinger, 1972.

Smith, Clark Ashton. *The Abominations of Yondo*. London: Neville Spearman, 1972.

————. *Genius Loci*. 1948; rpt. London: Neville Spearman, 1972.

————. *Lost Worlds*. 2 vols. 1944; rpt. London: Neville Spearman, 1971.

————. *Out of Space and Time*. 2 vols. 1942; rpt. London: Neville Spearman, 1971.

Stern, Philip Van Doren, ed. *Great Ghost Stories*. 1942; rpt. New York: Washington Square Press, 1947.

Stevenson, Robert Louis. *The Merry Men and Other Tales*. New York: Scribners, 1925. (A good edition of "The Strange Case of Dr. Jekyll and Mr. Hyde" can be found in the Buckler *Minor Masterpieces* anthology.)

Stoker, Bram. *The Bram Stoker Bedside Companion*. Charles Osborne, ed. New York: Taplinger, 1973.

Summers, Montague, ed. *The Supernatural Omnibus*. London: Gollancz, 1931.

————, ed. *Victorian Ghost Stories*. London: Simkin Marshall, 1934.

Swain, E. G. *The Stoneground Ghost Tales*. Cambridge: W. Heffer and Sons, 1912.

Wakefield, H. R. *The Clock Strikes Twelve*. 1946; rpt. New York: Ballantine, 1961.

————. *Ghost Stories*. London: Jonathan Cape, 1932.

————. *A Ghostly Company*. London: Jonathan Cape, 1935.

————. *Others Who Returned*. New York: Appleton, 1929.

————. *Strayers from Sheol*. Sauk City, Wis.: Arkham House, 1961.

————. *They Return at Evening*. New York: Appleton, 1928.

Walpole, Hugh. *All Souls' Night*. Garden City, N.Y.: Doubleday, Doran, 1933.

Wells, H. G. *Complete Short Stories*. London: Ernest Benn, 1927. St. Martin's edition, 1974, 22nd Impression.

Wharton, Edith. *The Ghost Stories of Edith Wharton*. New York: Scribner's, 1973.

Yeats, William Butler. *Mythologies*. 1959; rpt. New York: Collier, 1969.

SECONDARY SOURCES

Aickman, Robert. "Introduction." *The Fontana Book of Great Ghost Stories*. New York: Beagle, 1966.

Barzun, Jaques and Taylor, Wendell H. *A Catalogue of Crime*. New York: Harper and Row, 1971; Second Impression Corrected, 1974.

Beckett, Samuel. *Watt*. 1953; rpt. New York: Grove Press, 1959.

Begnal, Michael H. *Joseph Sheridan Le Fanu*. Lewisburg, Pa.: Bucknell University Press, 1971.

Benson, E. F. "Sheridan Le Fanu." *The Spectator*, 21 Feb., 1931, pp. 263-64.

Bien, Peter. *L. P. Hartley*. London: Chatto and Windus, 1963.

Blackwood, Algernon. "Preface." *Tales of Terror and the Unknown*. 1964; rpt. New York: Dutton, 1965.

Bleiler, E. F. *The Checklist of Fantastic Literature*. Chicago, Ill.: Shasta, 1948.

———. "Introduction." *Best Ghost Stories of Algernon Blackwood*. New York: Dover, 1973.

———. "Introduction." *Best Ghost Stories of J. S. Le Fanu*. New York: Dover, 1964.

Bloomfield, Paul. "L. P. Hartley." London: Longmans, Green, 1970.

Bowen, Elizabeth. "Introduction." J. S. Le Fanu. *The House by the Churchyard*. London: Blond, 1968.

Browne, Nelson. *Sheridan Le Fanu*. New York: Roy, 1951.

Buckler, William E. "Introduction." *Minor Classics of Nineteenth Century Fiction*. 2 vols. Boston: Riverside, 1967.

Davenport, Basil. "On Telling Stories." *Tales to be Told in the Dark*. New York: Dodd, Meade, 1953.

De Quincey, Thomas. "The Literature of Knowledge and the Literature of Power." *Thomas De Quincey*. Ed. Bonamy Dobre. New York: Schocken, 1965.

Edel, Leon. "Introduction." *Ghostly Tales of Henry James*. New York: Grossett and Dunlap, 1949.

———. "Introduction." Henry James. *Stories of the Supernatural*. New York: Taplinger, 1970.

Eliot, T. S. "Introduction." Charles Williams. *All Hallows Eve*. 1948; rpt. New York: Noonday, 1967.

Ellis, S. M. *Wilkie Collins, Le Fanu and Others*. London: Constable, 1931.

Ellmann, Richard. *Eminent Domain*. 1967; rpt. New York: Galaxy, 1970.

Fleming, Peter. "The Stuff of Nightmares." *Spectator Literary Supplement*, 18 April, 1931, p. 633.

Florescu, Radu and McNally, Raymond T. *In Search of Dracula*. New York: Warner, 1973.

Freud, Sigmund. *On Creativity and the Unconscious*. Ed. Benjamin Nelson. New York: Harper and Row, 1958.

"The Ghost Story: Folk Lore and the Literary Tale." *Morning Post*, 9 Feb., 1923, p. 11.

Gaselee, Stephen. M. R. James Obituary. *Proceedings of the British Academy*. XXII (1936), 424.

Harrison, John R. *The Reactionaries*. New York: Schocken, 1966.

Hartley, L. P. "Introduction." *The Third Ghost Book*. Ed. Cynthia Asquith. New York: Beagle, 1971.

Hill, John S. "The Dual Hallucination in 'The Fall of the House of Usher.'" *Southwest Review*. XLVII. (1963), 396-402.

Hitchcock, Alfred. "Preface." *Fourteen of My Favorites in Suspense*. New York: Dell, 1959.

Hudson, Derek. "A Study of Algernon Blackwood." *Essays and Studies*. London: John Murray, 1961.

Hynes, Samuel. *The Edwardian Turn of Mind*. 1968; rpt. Princeton, N. J.: Princeton University Paperbacks, 1971.

James, Henry. "The Liar." *The Short Stories of Henry James*. Ed. Clifton Fadiman. New York: Modern Library, 1945.

James, M. R. "Introduction." *Ghosts and Marvels*. London: Oxford University Press, 1927.

————. "Preface." *Ghost Stories of an Antiquary*. 1904; rpt. New York: Dover, 1971.

————. "Introduction." Joseph Sheridan Le Fanu. *Madam Crowl's Ghost*. London: G. Bell, 1923.

Kimbrough, Robert. "Backgrounds and Sources." Henry James. *The Turn of the Screw*. New York: Norton Critical, 1966.

Kirk, Russell. "A Cautionary Note on the Ghostly Tale." Russell Kirk. *The Surly Sullen Bell*. New York: Fleet, 1962.

Lawrence, T. E. Review of H. G. Wells's *Collected Stories*. *The Spectator*, 25 Feb., 1928, pp. 268-69.

Lovecraft, H. P. *Supernatural Horror in Literature*. 1927; rpt. New York: Dover, 1973.

Lubbock, S. G. *A Memoir of Montague Rhodes James*. Cambridge: Cambridge University Press, 1939.

Malden, R. H. "Preface." *Nine Ghosts*. London: Arnold, 1943.

Melville, Herman. "Hawthorne and his Mosses." *Moby Dick: Backgrounds and Sources*. Ed. Harrison Hayford, Hershel Parker. New York: Norton Critical, 1967.

Meng, Roderic, ed. "Books from Arkham House." Sauk City, Wis.: Arkham House, 1972.

Onions, Oliver. "Credo." *The Collected Ghost Stories of Oliver Onions*. New York: Dover, 1971.

Payn, James. *Some Literary Recollections*. New York: Harper, 1884.

Penzoldt, Peter. *The Supernatural in Fiction*. London: Peter Nevill, 1952.

Pfaff, William and Stillman, Edmund. *The Politics of Hysteria*. 1964; rpt. New York: Harper Colophon, 1965.

Pritchett, V. S. *The Living Novel and other Appreciations*. New York: Random House, 1964.

Sayers, Dorothy. "Introduction." *The Third Omnibus of Crime*. New York: Coward McCann, 1942.

Scarborough, Dorothy. *The Supernatural in Modern English Fiction*. 1917; rpt. New York: Octagon, 1967.

Stern, Philip Van Doren. "Introduction." *Great Ghost Stories*. 1942; rpt. New York: Washington Square Press, 1947.

————. "Introduction." Arthur Machen. *Tales of Horror and the Supernatural*. London: Richard Press, 1949.

Todorov, Tzetvan. *The Fantastic*. Ithaca, N.Y.: Cornell University Press, 1970.

Wakefield, H. R. "Farewell to All Those!" H. R. Wakefield. *Strayers from Sheol*. Sauk City, Wis.: Arkham House, 1961.

Waller, A. R. and Ward, A. W., eds. *The Cambridge History of English Literature*. Vol. XIV. Cambridge: Cambridge University Press, 1917.

Wilson, Edmund. *Classics and Commercials*. New York: Vintage, 1962.

Wolf, Leonard. *A Dream of Dracula*. New York: Popular Library, 1972.

Woolf, Virginia. "Henry James's Ghosts." *The Turn of the Screw: Backgrounds and Sources*. Ed. Robert Kimbrough. New York: Norton Critical, 1966.

INDEX